Decorating Baskets

Decorating Baskets

50 fabulous projects
using flowers, fabric,
beads, wire & more

Suzanne J. E.
Tourtillott

LARK BOOKS
A Division of Sterling Publishing Co., Inc.
New York

Art Director: **Kathleen Holmes**
Photography: **Evan Bracken**
Cover Design: **Barbara Zaretsky**
Illustrations: **Orrin Lundgren**
Assistant Editor: **Veronika Alice Gunter**
Editorial Assistance: **Rain Newcomb and Heather Smith**
Editorial Intern: **Anne Wolff Hollyfield**

Library of Congress Cataloging-in-Publication Data
Tourtillott, Suzanne J. E.
    Decorating baskets : 50 fabulous projects using flowers, fabric, beads, wire & more /
by Suzanne J. E. Tourtillott.
        p.   cm.
    Includes index.
    ISBN 1-57990-286-3
    1. Handicraft.   2. Baskets.   3. Decoration and Ornament.   I. Title
TT157 .T6296 2002
745.5—dc21
                                                    2001038071

10 9 8 7 6 5 4 3 2 1

Published by Lark Books, a division of
Sterling Publishing Co., Inc.
387 Park Avenue South, New York, N.Y. 10016

© 2002, Lark Books

Distributed in Canada by Sterling Publishing,
c/o Canadian Manda Group, One Atlantic Ave., Suite 105, Toronto, Ontario, Canada M6K 3E7

Distributed in the U.K. by:
Guild of Master Craftsman Publications Ltd.
Castle Place, 166 High Street, Lewes East Sussex, England BN7 1XU
Tel: (+ 44) 1273 477374, Fax: (+ 44) 1273 478606,
Email: pubs@thegmcgroup.com, Web: www.gmcpublications.com

Distributed in Australia by Capricorn Link (Australia) Pty Ltd., P.O. Box 704, Windsor, NSW 2756 Australia

If you have questions or comments about this book, please contact:
Lark Books
67 Broadway
Asheville, NC 28801
(828) 236-9730

Printed in China

ISBN 1-57990-286-3

CONTENTS

Introduction

Basics

Projects

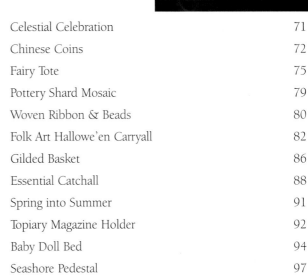

The Humble Basket
An Introduction

For centuries, people the world over have made and used baskets: ancient Egyptians wove them from palm leaves; Silk Road traders transported food and goods in them; and the Anasazi tribe carried their infants in two-legged ones.

There are many more kinds of baskets today than ever before! Traditionally, they're made from a variety of sturdy natural materials. Split oak, reed, twig, bamboo, wicker, and rattan are all typical basket materials, but there are now ingenious materials, such as metal and plastic, and new designs that combine wood, wire—even rope!—with traditional fibers. Baskets may have a rustic look or be sleekly modern. There are pedestal-footed baskets in sophisticated shapes made from natural materials and wire; you can easily feature one as a focal point on any table or shelf. What's more, with a little imagination and embellishment, you can customize your baskets to complement any room in your home, or simply beautify those baskets that are hard at work keeping your belongings in their place.

All of the projects in this book use simple baskets that you may own already, but you'll probably be inspired to buy more, once you find out how versatile and useful they can be. Why not cast a new eye on the humble, enduring basket?

BASICS

Decorating baskets is a creative endeavor that requires as little or as much time and work as you care to put into it. Whether you're crafting simple, last-minute gift baskets or creating decorated baskets for your home, you'll find all the basic information you need to create the extra-special baskets described in this book.

Anatomy of a Basket

Baskets, like sewing machines and beds, use the familiar names of body parts to name their various structural pieces. The *ribs* are the spokes (sometimes called *staves*) that rise from a basket's base. They cross the horizontal pieces, called *weavers*, to form the bowl. The place where the handle meets the rim, or *lip*, is called the *ear*.

Reinventing the Basket

Maybe you're not yet using baskets to their fullest. Sturdy reed and split-wood baskets are great for storing letters and magazines. Use smaller ones to store reading and writing accessories, or display your best garden tomatoes or fresh-baked bread on the dining table. Fill hanging wire baskets with oranges, onions, and potatoes in the kitchen, or with soaps, towels, and loofahs in the bathroom. Plastic baskets are handy for stashing toiletries. The newest metal baskets are highly versatile, and are fine for any room in the house.

You'll find it helpful to choose a basket with the right details for your design. One of your major considerations should be the quality of the basket's weave: is it open or tight? Flat or round? Open-weave designs let you wind all kinds of cord, wire, or ribbon through and around them, whether to secure other embellishments, or as the decorative motif itself. You can create bold arrangements, using sprays of foliage and flowers, with larger baskets. A tall, flat basket handle is a great place to apply decorative fabric and ribbon, and a broad rim can easily support three-dimensional items, such as artificial fruit and vegetables. A flat weave in the bowl of the basket will let you paint or découpage it with ease. Nearly all baskets, whether made of woven fiber or of wire, may be painted to suit your creative needs.

Look around your home—perhaps in the homes of your family and friends, or at flea markets—to find baskets deserving of your creative touch.

Supplies & Tools

Many of the methods shown for decorating your baskets use easy-to-find materials and tools, and just-as-easy craft techniques. Most of the tools you'll need are probably already in your home; what you don't have can be purchased at a craft supply store. Each project in this book comes complete with a short list of everything you'll need. When a project strikes your fancy, jot down the list. Collect the tools and materials you already have, then head out to the store. Once you're home, organize your work area, and put your tools into containers (how about some baskets?), for easy access.

Glue Gun

Once you've tried it, you'll wonder how you ever made crafts without it! It comes in sizes that range from mini to professional, and you can choose a gun that makes the glue hot, or merely warm. The glue gun holds a convenient pencil-size glue stick that melts a little bit at a time with a squeeze of the trigger. Apply the molten glue as it oozes from the gun's tip; it cools and hardens in a flash. You'll probably notice a few threads forming, as you pull the gun away from where you're applying the glue; just pull them off. Glue guns are not only perfect for attaching single flowers—or any lightweight item—to your basket, they make quick work of putting fabric or trims in place, too.

COLD GLUES & ADHESIVES

For the best results, use the glue that is suitable for the materials you're working with. For

Left to right: Glue sticks, craft glue, cyanoacrylate glue, spray adhesives, glue gun

découpage and decorative other techniques, craft (PVA) glue, an inexpensive white household glue, works well and dries with a clear finish. Some spray adhesives, which are very clean and fast to use, allow you to reposition the item; there are even sprays appropriate for fabric, so that you can "sew" without needle or thread. Use spray adhesives only in well-ventilated rooms, directed over a piece of scrap paper, for lightweight jobs. Use wood or carpenter's glue when applying motifs to wooden surfaces. If you're repairing a basket, wire or clamp the pieces together before applying the appropriate adhesive, and let the glue set overnight.

WIRE

You'll find that floral stems and other similarly shaped objects should be wired or tied, rather than glued, to your basket. Wire is strong and secure; it can be passed through the basket's weave, or around the handle; and you can use it to bind bundles of florals or foliage. Use wire to create a hanging loop if you want to turn a flat basket into a wall hanging, such as the Wedding Memories basket on page 99. A light gauge (the higher the number, the finer the wire) is fine for most uses. Use green floral wire (it's easy to hide) for dried and silk flowers.

SEALERS

Use a sealer to protect a painted or découpaged basket from dirt and wear. Shellacs and varnishes are applied with brush or spray, dry to a clear finish, and prevent discoloration of the images, but be aware that shellac may discolor certain gilding products. Spray acrylic sealants come in matte, satin, and glossy finishes, are suitable for most hard surfaces, and are by far the most convenient to use.

PAINTBRUSHES

A variety of small sizes will be useful. Use bristle brushes when you want a satiny smooth finish, and invest in the better quality kind because it's no fun trying to remove a stray hair once it's caught in glue or varnish. Use mineral spirits to remove oil-based paints from brushes, or use convenient latex paints that clean up with soap and water. Foam paintbrushes are super-simple, inexpensive, and disposable; they'll do the trick for many craft techniques.

SANDPAPER & STEEL WOOL

If your basket has a varnish or sealer already on it, you may need to prepare the surface by sanding it smooth before gluing or painting it. Both of these abrasives are available in several grades for wood or metal; start with a coarse grade and finish the job with a very fine one.

CUTTING TOOLS & AIDS

You'll need a variety of cutting tools, such as a craft knife, scissors, and wire cutters. A craft knife is perfect to cut out a border, or any intricate detail, but use a metal straightedge with the knife if you want a perfectly straight line. Replace the knife's blade as soon as it gets dull, and keep the protective cap on it when it's not in use. A thick piece of cardboard can serve as a cutting mat, to protect other surfaces.

The sharper your scissors, the better. It's a good idea to use different scissors for paper and fabric; they'll cut better and stay sharper longer. Spring-handled pliers with a built-in wire cutter, available in craft stores, will help you securely twist, wrap, and cut the floral wire that is often used to hold floral stems and other medium-weight accents.

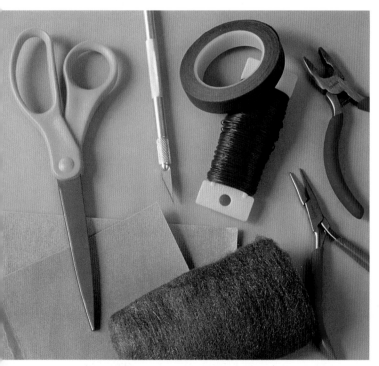

Left to right: Scissors, craft knife, floral tape, floral wire, wire cutters, spring-handled pliers, steel wool, sandpaper

TECHNIQUES & IDEAS

You're probably familiar with many of the following decorative techniques, but here's a quick review, along with some information that may be new to you.

FABRIC FOR ALL REASONS

Fabric softens the lines of a basket, and will make your baskets stand out with a versatile decorator's touch. A veil of sheer cloth can add drama to a ho-hum basket. A lightweight printed cotton lining is perfect for a doll basket, such as the Baby Doll Bed shown on page 94 (don't be surprised if your cat likes to curl up inside!). Try trimming your basket with a fabric skirt—it's an easy way to dress up a working basket without reducing its storage capacity, and you can change the skirt to suit the season or the décor of new surroundings. Although you'll need a sewing machine, some basic sewing skills, and a few embroidery stitches for some of the projects, you may be surprised to learn that you needn't get out the needle and thread in order to use fabrics in

Fabrics on baskets can range from bright printed cottons and woven patterns...

...to luxe fabrics like velvet and lamé.

10

all your baskets. The Pure and Simple Vintage Basket, page 24, cleverly uses glue instead. The following tips will walk you through a variety of ways to decorate baskets with fabric.

Linings in a Flash

Linings are so practical, yet make the basket so much more special. It's easy to fit the fabric to the basket by folding darts in the corners, or by arranging a series of softly gathered pleats.

You can secure the darts or pleats with needle and thread, a sewing machine—even hot glue! For light fabrics, hot glue the darts or pleats in place in the basket. Instead of pinnning and basting an outer fabric and a liner fabric together, try one of the new aerosol basting sprays before stitching. Toto's Picnic Basket (page 114), with its bandana-print twill lining, pops out of the basket for a quick switch, or for cleaning.

Skirt Your Basket

For the simplest kind of fabric skirt, first measure the circumference of your basket's rim, and cut a length of fabric about twice as long. Sew the side seam together and press it open. Fold over a top hem and press it neatly down. Create gathers with loose running stitches or with elastic. Sew and press the skirt's bottom hem (or use that wonderful basting spray!). If your basket's rim has slopes or curves, you'll need to mark the hem with pins or chalk to ensure evenness. Attach the skirt to the basket's outside rim with hot glue, and add accents of ribbon or lace with hot glue. For new inspiration, see the Fairy Tote on page 75; it has a wonderfully creative fabric "collar" (using ribbon drawstrings) that miraculously expands the capacity of the basket.

RIBBONS! RIBBONS! RIBBONS!

Ribbon imparts charm and finish to almost any basket. Whether you want a simple or elaborate effect, it's often the color, texture, and placement of ribbon that can really give you the look you want. You can find lace, organza, polyester, silk, velvet, cotton, paper, and even mesh ribbon in a variety of colors, patterns, and widths. Ribbon with woven edges is used for sewing as well as for crafting; ribbon with cut edges is treated with a fabric stiffener and is suited for crafting only. Wired ribbon holds its shape beautifully, so your bows never go flat.

You can also use other material in the same way as you do ribbon; think of using crepe paper streamers, scarves, cord, raffia, or any starched or stiffened cloth. Whatever you use as ribbon material, you can drape it, twist it, roll it, weave it, sew it on with needle and thread, glue it on in a few strategic places, or tie it in a bow.

Many bows can themselves be embellished. You might festoon the center with a small vintage brooch or button, for a special touch. For ideas on other bow-related adornments, see the section on Dried Flowers, Silk Flowers, & Whimsies, on page 15.

Bows add pizzazz! Choose from a fantastic array of ribbon materials, then tie your own unique creation.

Bow Tying 101

Here are tips for making lush, creative bows from almost any ribbon material. Remember to make the bow proportionate to the size and shape of your basket. For the fullest bows, use plenty of ribbon.

• Double Shoelace Bow •

1. Cut a 12-inch (30.5 cm) piece of ribbon. Fold it down to form a loop, with the two ends overlapping

in the back. Cut another length of ribbon about 2 inches (5 cm) smaller. Place the second ribbon on top of the first. Cut another piece of ribbon the same size as the second piece and fold it over the two loops, from back to front; see figure 1.

Fig. 1

2. Tie the third ribbon around the two loops into a knot. Pull it tight and slide the knot around to the back, as shown in figure 2.

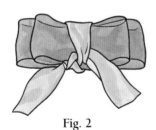

Fig. 2

3. Cut each end of the dangling ribbon into a V, or fishtail. Fluff the loops into a pleasing shape.

4. Secure the bow to your basket with hot glue, or string a piece of wire or thread through the knot in the back, and tie it to the ribbon on the basket.

• Shoelace Bow •

This classic is especially charming when you use wired ribbon.

1. Cut a long piece of ribbon. Cut the ends into a V, or fishtail, as shown in figure 1.

Fig. 1

2. Make a loop out of the left end of the ribbon, leaving a tail, and loop the right side underneath the ribbon and back over the top again; see figure 2.

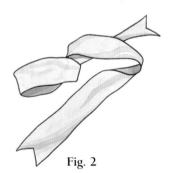

Fig. 2

3. Referring to figure 3, slip a loop from the right side of the ribbon through the folded-over part of the ribbon.

4. Pull the loop through the knot completely, making sure that both sides are even. Fluff the bow.

Fig. 3

• Double Bow •

Try using two types of coordinated ribbon material that complement each other.

1. Cut two ribbons the same length. (Longer ribbon and more loops will create a fuller, rounder bow.) Zigzag the first ribbon and place the second ribbon on top of the first, also looped back and forth, from right to left (see figure 1).

2. Gather the ribbon loops together flat, and tie a thin gold wire ribbon or gold cord around the middle, as shown in figure 2.

3. Push the knotted gold ribbon to the back of the bow and fluff the loops so that they form a circular shape.

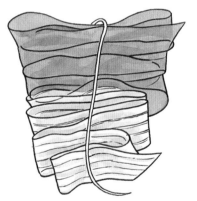

Fig. 1

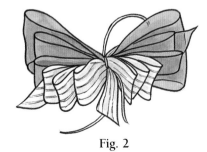

Fig. 2

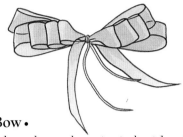

• Multi-Bow •

This quick and easy bow is tied with a bit of gold cord.

1. Cut a long piece of ribbon, approximately 36 inches (91 cm) long. Zigzag the ribbon into loops, making the loops longer at the top and narrower at the bottom, as shown in figure 1.

2. Bring the loops together and tie them in the middle with a piece of thin gold wire ribbon or cord; see figure 2. Move the knot to the back of the bow.

3. Separate the loops from each other, so that each loop is visible. Trim the tails to an equal length.

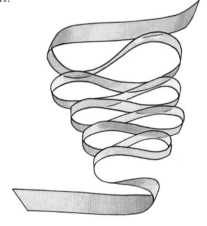

Fig. 1

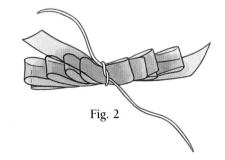

Fig. 2

13

DÉCOUPAGE WITH FABRIC OR PAPER

Découpage is the art of decorating a surface with scraps or cutouts of printed images, using a clear, flexible adhesive, such as découpage medium, craft glue, or acrylic gesso. Look for baskets made

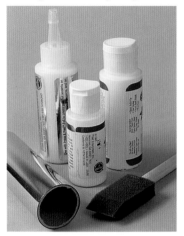

Découpage and gilding are just two of the many quick and simple ways to transform plain baskets

from split wood, or those with a tight weave. Pre-treated decals are available in craft stores, or you can make your own from any sort of printed material, including postcards and greeting cards, wrapping paper, old maps, drawings; embossed and decorative papers will work, too. Mail-order companies and select shops sell reproductions of traditional découpage images, in black and white or with hand-tinted color added, or you can use watercolors and pencils on them for your own one-of-a-kind look. Keep a file of the printed images that you find, so you'll have them when you're ready to découpage a basket.

Novelty printed fabrics broaden the range of possibilities for découpage; you can see these on the Teddy Bear Toy Holder, on page 43. Even dried and pressed natural materials, such as dried flowers, leaves, grass, and bark, often make excellent découpage material; for more inspiration, turn to Autumn Leaves on page 21. For an unusual art-gallery look, such as the Handmade Paper Découpage Basket on page 56, cover a closely woven basket with torn sheets of handmade paper.

Select an image and carefully cut it out; coat a small area on the basket with acrylic gesso or découpage medium, using a bristle or foam paintbrush. Next, lay the cutout or torn piece onto the wet area. Smooth each piece against the basket with the brush. Let it dry—it doesn't take long. Finish with several coats of découpage medium or acrylic gesso for a protective finish. The Topiary Magazine basket, page 92, is another great example of this easy decorative method.

THE NATURAL WAY

Nature offers an enormous variety of wonderful objects with which you can embellish your baskets. Keep your eyes open for leaves, dried flowers, pressed or fresh flowers, twigs, feathers, pods, grasses, acorns, nuts, and fresh and dried fruit…anyone can increase the list! As a bonus, many natural herbs and flowers keep their fragrance even after they've dried. Some treasures, like the seashells on the Seashore Pedestal (page 97), are ready to use just as you find them, but botanicals may need some special attention. To

A wide selection of dried natural materials is at your fingertips

make them flat enough for découpage, press flowers and leaves between blotting sheets and heavy books. For sprays and stems, spread them out on paper in a dark, dry, well-ventilated area for drying. Drying time varies from a few days to several weeks, depending on the density and moisture of the materials. Silica gel, available at many floral shops, speeds the drying process of natural materials to just a few days.

DRIED FLOWERS, SILK FLOWERS & WHIMSIES

Dried flowers, silk flowers, and small novelty items are popular for decorating baskets. Dried and silk flowers are especially well suited for adorning the handles and rims, such as the Winterberry Christmas basket on page 117. Whimsies and miniatures add a distinctive touch to a basket and are great for personalizing a gift basket; turn to page 121 to see the New Baby basket, adorned with tiny alphabet blocks and paper flowers.

Often you'll want to select items that suit the room where the basket will be displayed, such as plastic or papier-mâché fruit and vegetables for the kitchen; see the To Market, To Market basket, on page 48, for a charming example. For a gift basket with a special theme, you'll have no trouble finding just the right novelty item for embellishment, be it a single silk magnolia blossom or a handsome collection of gilded seed pods.

Floral moss is often used in combination with dried flowers. Both of these types of embellishments adhere quickly with a glue gun, and benefit from an annual misting with regular hair spray. To decorate with moss, apply a short section of hot glue to the basket's rim, and twist the moss into a tight strip, molding the moss into place; the springy material will expand a bit once it's adhered.

Avoid displaying dried flowers in damp areas or near heat sources. They can absorb moisture, and they're flammable.

Choose from the many artificial fruit, vegetables, and flowers…

…some so realistic that they rival dried naturals.

BEADING

Beads are the perfect adornment for a wire basket. Hundreds of tiny beads can add a delicate and complex quality, and a few large handblown glass ones can be as bold and distinctive as the basket itself. Translucent beads glimmer and reflect light.

Wood, plastic, and glass beads are fine for baskets. Use thin, flexible beading wire and a beading needle for the smallest beads.

Wood and bone beads might suggest a rustic or primitive look. Fashion hangers from wire to set the beads apart from the basket, where they'll dramatically catch the light.

For inspiration, look at the Glass Dangles Wire Pedestal on page 60. There are many other ways to use beads for decoration, too. Wire them directly to a basket, or sew them onto a fabric skirt or liner. Glue them on for a fun, casual look, as seen on the Retro Daisies basket on page 36. No matter what kind of beads you choose, the technique for stringing is simple. Here are just a few ideas to get you started:

How to String Beads

Be sure the beads you choose have large enough holes to accommodate the stringing material. String beads on ribbon, thread, leather, or wire. Drape, hang, or weave the strung beads into your basket. For seed beads, use a beading needle with beading thread to make the job easier. Pull the thread gently to remove kinks in it, then secure each end with a knot.

Wire baskets are especially suited to wired beads; the Beaded Home Décor on page 27 uses a simple wiring technique to transform an ordinary metal wire basket into a stunning centerpiece. Just choose the appropriate gauge of beading wire, and use spring-handled pliers to make a small loop (rather than a knot) in one end, to keep the beads in place.

For an interesting effect called *couching*, lay down prestrung beads on fabric to create or embellish lines of the design, then stitch over them with more thread to secure. You might add a second thread of beads on top for extra texture. A more casual beading technique, using tiny seed beads randomly sewn onto fabric, adorns the Fairy Tote on page 75.

STAMPING

Stamping is an easy way to quickly add visual interest to a basket. Prepare the surface of the basket by sealing or painting it first. A huge variety of stamps and ink pad colors are available at most craft

Baskets can be painted, or you can use rubber stamping techniques.

supply stores. The simplest of stamps can be made with items that are found in your home and yard. Small fruits and vegetables have inherently interesting shapes that make them a natural for printing. Slice a vegetable, such as a mushroom, in half, then dab it with a paper towel to remove excess moisture. You now have a simple stamp that you can ink and print! Embellish your stamped designs with paint pens, gilding, or antiquing solutions. Spray with an aerosol sealant to protect the design from dirt and wear.

COLOR TREATMENTS

Get just the right color in a new basket, give an old basket a new look, or completely revamp a flea market find with one of the many color products available. Sponging provides an interesting textured finish on a plain or painted basket. Fabric dyes offer deep-toned color without splatters or fumes. Metallic finishes can look brightly up-to-date or have an aged, antique appearance. Here are some quick tips for coloring techniques.

Painting

Tubes, cans, spray—when it comes to paint, you have a wide range of options. Each formulation has its own special characteristics, but some are better suited for basket painting than others. Particularly porous basket materials, such as raw wood, should be prepared with primer first. Use the type of primer (water- or oil-based) that is best suited for your paint type. Many baskets that appear to have a natural finish are actually varnished, so test the paint's compatibility on the underside of the basket's base if you're not sure. It's a good idea to seal a basket once you've finished; for more information, read about Sealers on page 9.

• Acrylic & Latex •

Quick-drying, water-based acrylic and latex paints are available in small cans and tubes. You can mix them for custom effects, adding white to make pastel colors, and black or brown for darker shades. The soap-and-water cleanup is quick and easy. Aerosol sprays are most convenient, and they come in a rainbow of colors.

• Oil & Alkyd •

Artist's oils in tubes are more expensive than the paint that comes in cans and sprays, so use them sparingly. They're slow-drying, and should be thinned with linseed oil or another suitable substance. Clean your brushes with mineral spirits. You can use an oil paint as a dark undercoat, or *bole*, for gilding with metal leaf (see Gilding, page 18).

Alkyds are oil-based paints that come in matte, eggshell, and gloss finishes, and they can be thinned with mineral spirits or other solvents; be sure to wait 24 hours between coats.

• Enamel •

Available in aerosol sprays and small cans, these paints come in a wide range of colors and are best used on metal, following a primer coat (even on already-painted metal). Enamels don't dry as quickly as acrylics, but be sure to apply several light coats for even, dripless color, and finish with a clear spray sealant.

PAINT TECHNIQUES

Change the look of an unfinished basket in a flash by using one of these easy processes.

Washes and Glazes

Get subtle textural effects and enhance the color of the base coat by applying a second coat of diluted paint. If this second coat is a lighter color, it's called a wash; a glaze is darker than the base coat. Start with a clean, dry basket, and apply an aerosol sealer coat; allow it to dry. Next, apply the base coat; for best results, use a small brush with natural bristles for all of the paint coats. Here are some guidelines for mixing your wash or glaze paints:

> **Wash:** Three parts thinner or solvent to one part white and one part base color paints
>
> **Glaze:** Three parts thinner or solvent to one part black and one part base color paints

Apply your wash or glaze to the basket, starting on the inside and working from top to bottom. After a few minutes, use an absorbent, lint-free cloth to gently wipe off the excess paint. Leave the wash or glaze deposits in the recessed areas on the basket. When dry, apply a clear coat of aerosol varnish.

DYEING & STAINING

To dye a wicker basket, use ordinary fabric dye (the liquid form is easier to mix than the powder; both are widely available in stores). Prepare the dye according to the package instructions. For a nice mottled effect, brush on one to three coats of dye, depending on the intensity of color you like. For deep, solid color, dilute the dye in a pot large enough to hold the basket. Immerse the basket in the dye until it's just slightly lighter than the intensity you want. It will dry somewhat darker than it appears when wet. Use rubber gloves and a pair of non-food plastic tongs to remove or turn the wet basket. After it's dried on a flattened paper bag, apply a sealer coat.

You can stain baskets in much the same way you'd stain a piece of furniture. Of course, stains are best suited to split-wood baskets, but you can test the product on the underside of any raw, unfinished material. It's best to apply a stain with a brush or wadded-up cheesecloth, since some glues that hold baskets together may dissolve when exposed to a lot of the liquid.

GILDING

Gleaming precious-metal finishes on baskets kick them up a notch! The beautiful Gilded Basket on page 86 used composition leaf to give it a warm, golden glow.

Leaf

The quick-and-easy gilding products available at craft stores use composition-metal leaf, which comes in a variety of bright and antiqued metal finishes such as gold, copper, and silver. With composition leaf, you can get nearly the same beautiful look as the real gold leaf that fine craftsmen use, but it's much more cost effective.

First, seal the basket's surface with acrylic gesso; use shellac to seal the raw, porous wood used in market baskets. For metal, use a bonding liquid (available in cans or sprays) as a primer coat. Apply a dark undercoat (either oil or acrylic) and let it dry. You may be able to use the undercoat itself as a sealer, if the basket's surface is not too porous or rough. Next, apply an oil- or water-based *size*, according to the manufacturer's directions, with a foam brush. When it dries to the tack stage, it's time to apply the leaf. Lay small pieces of leaf in position, and gently rub the backing tissue into place with a smooth wad of cotton knit, or, for rougher surfaces, use a stencil brush. Let the leaf dry for the amount of time recommended by the size's manufacturer, then remove the backing, and brush off any loose or excess leaf with a soft brush. Use an acrylic spray sealer for light protection to keep the leaf from tarnishing.

WATERPROOFING

If you plan to display your finished baskets outdoors, you'll need to waterproof them after painting them. Apply two thin coats of varnish, followed by a coat of waterproofing medium from a paint store. Allow each coat to dry completely before adding the next.

GIVE A GREAT GIFT BASKET

A gift basket is a wonderfully stylish way to celebrate, congratulate, or applaud a special occasion. This type of basket lets you decorate with extra details that relate to the theme or event, and then you can fill it with a collection of small gifts that are sure to delight the recipient. For a bon voyage gift, you might start by embellishing the basket with bright, metallic streamers and paper party hats, then line it with a pair of fine linen napkins. Fill the basket with a pair of plastic champagne glasses, a split of bubbly, and packs of fancy imported snacks like caviar and crackers (be sure to tuck in a copy of a guide to their destination, too!). Once you get rolling, you'll find that there are plenty of thoughtful ways to decorate a gift basket that says, "You're special."

INSPIRATION

In this book, five talented designers present their wonderfully creative ideas for decorating baskets. Their designs are truly innovative, and the step-by-step instructions will tell you how to achieve the very same look. Feel free to modify the colors of the material to complement your home décor. Before you know it, you'll be coming up with your own designs.

Now it's time to see just how inspiring decorating baskets can be!

Autumn Leaves

DESIGNER: CORINNE KURZMANN

The earthy colors of autumn leaves are a simple and natural complement to any simple rustic basket. Designer Corinne Kurzmann used découpage techniques to adhere pressed fall foliage to this tightly woven container.

WHAT YOU'LL NEED

Large basket with a tight weave

Pressed dried leaves

Powdered découpage medium

Medium-sized artist's paintbrush

Small container with lid

Wet rag

INSTRUCTIONS

1. Collect an assortment of leaves, and dry them by placing them between sheets of newspaper under a heavy book for several days. You can use the same technique to dry flowers.

2. Assemble your dried leaves on a work surface in an attractive arrangement for your basket.

3. Mix the découpage powder with water, following the manufacturer's directions, until it has a smooth paste consistency.

4. Carefully brush the découpage paste onto the back of a leaf and press it against the basket where desired. Hold each leaf in place for several seconds, until it adheres to the basket. Keep a wet rag handy for wiping your hands as you work with the leaves and sticky paste.

5. Once all of the leaves are positioned, brush a light layer of the découpage paste over the arrangement, for a protective finish. The paste will appear white, but it will dry clear. Let dry for approximately one hour, then apply another coat of découpage paste.

Jeweled Wire Tray

DESIGNER: TERRY TAYLOR

These smart, functional woven-wire baskets really need little decoration,
but they become playfully elegant with the addition of glass "jewels."

WHAT YOU'LL NEED

- Woven wire basket
- Glass jewels
- 24-gauge steel wire
- Flat-nose jewelry pliers
- Wire cutters

INSTRUCTIONS

1. Use the wire cutters to cut several lengths of the 24-gauge wire, each 8 inches (20.3 cm) in length. Set them aside.

2. Determine the placement of the glass jewels. You might make a single row, or dot them randomly around the basket.

3. Tightly wind one end of a length of 24-gauge wire around a weaver. Hold the jewel with your thumb or forefinger. Wind the wire diagonally across the jewel, wrap it tightly around a weaver, and bring it around behind the jewel.

4. Wrap the wire tightly around the weaver at the opposite side. Hold onto the jewel with your finger to keep it from popping out. Bring up the wire to the opposite corner and wrap it tightly around a weaver. Trim the wire with the wire cutters.

5. Repeat steps 3 and 4 for each jewel.

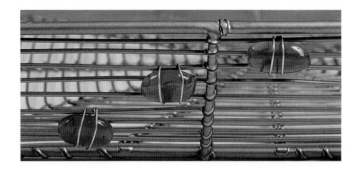

PURE & SIMPLE VINTAGE BASKET

DESIGNER: JEAN TOMASO MOORE

The secret to returning vintage fabrics to a pristine white is to gently bleach and starch them. Here, fanciful vintage buttons add the perfect embellishment.

WHAT YOU'LL NEED

Shaker style basket (this oblong one, made from wide woven reed, measures 13 inches [33 cm] in length)

Paintbrush

White satin-finish latex enamel paint

Cloth measuring tape

1 yard (.9 m) vintage (or new) lace (for this project an old pillow case with hand crocheted lace border was used)

Scissors

Iron and ironing board

Glue gun with glue sticks

20 vintage bone and pearl buttons in various sizes and shades of white

Ecru lace trim, 2 inches (5 cm) wide, with a pale yellow satin ribbon woven through the center; for this project, a 20-inch (50.8 cm) length was needed to cover the basket's handle

INSTRUCTIONS

1. Paint the basket white.

2. Measure the circumference of the basket's rim. Cut a length of the lace crochet long enough to encircle the basket's rim. If you use a lace-edged piece of fabric, leave 2 inches (5 cm) of

the fabric connected to the lace. Allow enough extra length to be able to turn and press one raw edge of the fabric under for a neat finish.

3. Fold over the raw edge of the fabric and press it flat, to create a crisp edge.

4. Starting at the base of the handle, glue the folded and ironed long edge of the fabric all around the top rim of the basket. Fold over one end of the piece where it meets and overlaps itself, and glue it down; this creates a finished seam.

5. Glue the buttons onto the fabric at the rim of the basket. Glue several buttons vertically over the seam of the fabric to help hide it.

6. Lay the ecru lace trim over the handle. Place a bead of hot glue along the underside of the handle, and fold the edges of the trim under the handle on each side. The trim should completely cover the handle.

7. Glue a button or two at the inside base ends of the handle, if desired, for further accent.

Beaded Home Décor

DESIGNER: CORINNE KURZMANN

Tiny seed beads on an ordinary wire basket make a stunning centerpiece. You'll love the way the multicolored beads shift in color with the changing light.

WHAT YOU'LL NEED

Wire basket with vertical ribs

32-gauge wire

Wire cutters

Size 10 seed beads, 1½ cups (330 g)

Scissors

3 yards (2.7 m) embroidered silk ribbon

Glue gun and glue sticks

1¼ yards (1.1 m) orange ribbon

Lots of patience and time

INSTRUCTIONS

1. Cut the wire into plenty of 12-inch (30.5 cm) lengths. You can cut more as needed.

2. To keep the beads from falling off, fold one end of a length of wire into a small loop. String the beads onto the wire, leaving a 3-inch (7.6 cm) tail of bare wire; loop this end.

3. Starting at the bottom, gently wrap one end of the bare wire around the spokes of the basket. Stretch the wire across to the next rib. At each intersection of

the basket, wrap the beaded wire around the rib, moving the beads to the outside, so the wire on the inside of the rib remains bare. When you reach the end of the strand, wrap the end of the bare wire around the nearest rib and trim the end closely, to hide it. Continue to wrap lengths of beaded wire onto the basket until it's completely covered.

4. Wrap the rim completely, weaving over and under it with the beaded wire.

5. To cover the exposed wire ribs on the inside of the basket, cut a length of ribbon for each one. Hot glue them into place.

6. If the basket has a base, hot glue a length of ribbon onto it.

7. Weave the orange ribbon in and out of the sections at the top of the basket. Tie a multi-bow; see Bow Tying 101 on page 13 for more information.

South of the Border Basket

DESIGNER: ALLISON SMITH

Pile the salsa chips high in this stunning design, which easily serves as a grand centerpiece or serving basket at a buffet.

WHAT YOU'LL NEED

Shallow grapevine basket with a single handle

Raffia

Scissors

Two bunches of artificial chili peppers

INSTRUCTIONS

1. Gather a handful of raffia and tie into a shoelace bow (for more information, see Bow Tying 101, page 12).

2. Carefully thread the wire stem of the chili pepper bunch through the raffia at the back side of the center knot.

3. Push the wire through the base of the handle and wrap tightly to secure it. If the base of the basket handle is too tight to accommodate the wire, attach the raffia and peppers with a small length of wire.

4. Repeat steps 1 through 3 on the other side of the basket handle.

VARIATION

Change the flavor completely by using artificial pears and apples instead; accent them with a cheery plaid wired ribbon.

Sophisticated Gift Wine Baskets

DESIGNER: ALLISON SMITH

So much more stylish than a brown paper bag! Decorated gift baskets for a housewarming, a dinner party, or a celebration of any kind make what's inside even more special.

What You'll Need

- 2 loosely woven wine baskets
- 2 wine labels (see step 1; soak off from old bottles before recycling)
- 2 small sheets of decorative paper, to coordinate with the wine labels
- Glue stick
- Scissors
- Gold thread
- Gold glaze (purchase at a craft store, or mix thinning medium with gold paint)
- Corded tassel
- Foam paintbrush
- Black satin ribbon, 54 inches (1.4 m) in length

Instructions

1. Soak the bottles in a pot of very hot water for about 20 minutes. The labels should slide right off. Allow the labels to dry, then press them flat with a warm iron.

2. To determine the size of the card, position each label on a sheet of the decorative paper. Cut the paper to a slightly larger size and a shape proportionate to the label. Use the glue stick to attach the wine label to the paper. Make a small hole in the corner and tie on a gold thread for the hanger.

3. Paint the basket with two coats of gold glaze. Allow to dry.

4. Attach the gift tag with the corded tassel. For the second basket, weave the satin ribbon through the basket and attach the gift tag. Tie the ribbon in a loose, floppy bow.

CHROME BATH & SHOWER BASKET

DESIGNER: ALLISON SMITH

Colorful craft wire is the only decorative element needed for a waterproof designer look in the bath. This basket makes a great tote for favorite shampoos and other personal care accessories.

WHAT YOU'LL NEED

Chrome basket

18-gauge copper wire, 48 feet (14.4 m) in length (wire amounts will vary with the size of your basket)

18-gauge anodized wire in various colors, 48 feet (14.4 m) in length (wire amounts will vary with the size of your basket)

Needle-nose pliers

Wire cutters

INSTRUCTIONS

1. Working with 48-inch (1.2 m) lengths of wire, wrap the wire around small sections of the basket in a random checkerboard pattern. Use the pliers to pull the wire tightly against the basket, then clip and weave each wire end under the already-wrapped wire to secure it.

VARIATION

As you're wrapping the wire around the basket's ribs, add an interesting bead to every other section.

BOTANICAL BASKET

DESIGNER: TERRY TAYLOR

*Horticulturists, brush up on your botanical names! Make this easy
basket for a favorite potted plant.*

WHAT YOU'LL NEED

Straight-sided basket with wide ribs

Paintbrush

Acrylic paint, pale green

Acrylic paint pen, medium shade of green

Horticultural dictionary or gardening book
    with plant list

Rubber stamp alphabet

Rubber stamp pad

Rubber stamp with floral motif; we used
    a leaf shape

Accent pen

INSTRUCTIONS

1. Give your basket a coat of pale green paint, both inside and out. Let the first coat dry, and give it a second coat if needed.

2. Accent the basket with the paint pen in a medium shade of green. Let it dry.

3. Measure the length of your basket's ribs. This will be the amount of space that you have to rubber stamp your plant names on. Line up several of your rubber stamp letters to determine how many letters you can stamp on a rib. In the project illustrated, no more than seven or eight letters would fit there.

4. Consult a horticultural dictionary or a plant list to find flower names that contain the appropriate number of letters. Don't be stymied if your favorite flower—fritillaria—won't fit; you'll be amazed at the sheer number of plant names you have to choose from. Write down the plant names. (I guarantee you won't remember all of them or their correct spelling!)

5. Stamp a plant name on a rib. If you make a mistake, quickly moisten a paper towel and wipe off your mistake. Re-stamp the letter. Skip a rib and stamp the next plant name. Repeat around the basket.

6. Stamp a simple floral or leaf motif on the ribs you skipped. Vary the placement of the stamp. Highlight the stamp, if desired, using an accent pen.

7. Fill the basket with a potted plant for a quick gift.

RETRO DAISIES

DESIGNER: TERRY TAYLOR

Give the 1960s' daisy motif another go-go with easy-to-use craft foam and chunky plastic beads. Just a few daisies on a bright basket are guaranteed to bring on spring in a hurry.

What You'll Need

- Blue basket with handle
- Blue acrylic paint (optional)
- Paintbrush (optional)
- Sheets of craft foam, bright green and white
- Stapler (optional)
- Scissors
- Sewing needle
- Beading or sewing thread
- Yellow plastic beads
- Glue gun and glue sticks

Instructions

1. The basket was already painted a bright sky blue. Craft and discount stores are usually well stocked with brightly painted baskets. If your basket is unpainted, paint it now with acrylic paint.

2. Copy the template (see figure 1). Enlarge and reduce the template on a photocopier as desired. Three sizes of daisies adorn this basket. Make several copies.

3. You may find it easier to cut out the daisies if you staple the center of the petal template to the white craft foam. Use the scissors to cut out as many petal shapes as you wish, and set them aside.

4. Cut out circles for the centers from the bright green foam. Set them aside.

Fig. 1

5. Thread your needle with a 12-inch (30.5 cm) length of thread. Knot one end. Use a small stitch to attach the center to the petal. Then stitch several yellow beads, one at a time, scattered over the center circle. Knot the end and trim the thread. Repeat for each daisy you've cut out.

6. Hot-glue the beaded daisies to the basket handle and the portion of the basket close to where the handle joins the basket body.

Variation

Craft foam is available in precut fun shapes, too. Choose the basket, and the foam colors and figures, to complement your theme.

BRASS TACKS

DESIGNER: TERRY TAYLOR

*The simple brass nails that attach the handles of this basket to the
rim were the inspiration for this spare and—dare we say—masculine
approach to decorating baskets.*

WHAT YOU'LL NEED

- Basket with broad, flat rim
- Brass-colored craft studs
- Glue gun and glue sticks (optional)

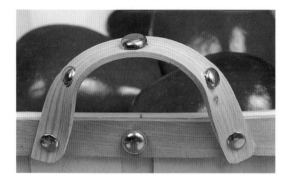

INSTRUCTIONS

1. Plan the layout of the studs you chose. It's easy to simply arrange the studs along the base of the basket and move them about as needed. Careful planning will prevent you from making excessive marks in the rim if you push in a stud and have to remove it.

2. Use firm, even pressure to press the studs into the basket rim. If you need additional support, rest the inner rim of the basket against a corner of a table. Press hard against the table, and the stud will be seated well.

VARIATION

If your basket rim is thick, you could use decorative upholstery tacks. For a bright, cheery look with a little color, use brightly painted thumbtacks around the rim

Veggie Lunch Tote

DESIGNER: ALLISON SMITH

Perk up a workday lunch or a Saturday jaunt with this spacious fabric-lined basket.
Don't forget to add an apple and a magazine!

What You'll Need

Medium-sized two-handle basket

Coordinating fabric for 2 ties, cut as
  described below

Scissors

Sewing machine

Coordinating thread

Fabric to double-line the inside of the basket,
  plus a 3-inch (7.6 cm) overhang all around

Iron

Instructions

1. Make the ties. Cut two strips of material 5 inches (12.7 cm) wide and long enough to wrap around the basket. Be sure to add enough extra length to be able to tie a generous bow on either side of the basket. With the right sides together, fold the fabric in half lengthwise. Sew one end and the entire side of the fabric. Turn the fabric right side out by placing the end on the handle of a wooden spoon and pushing it through. Press the sash. Finish the open end by folding the raw edges under, and whipstich the opening closed. Repeat with the other fabric strip.

2. Fold the remaining fabric in half with the right sides together. Carefully smooth and tuck the fabric into the basket to create a lining. Keep the fabric positioned so that the gathers lie evenly around the sides of the basket. Drape the excess material over the sides, and trim where necessary for an even 3-inch (7.6 cm) overhang all the way around the basket. Pin the edges of the fabric together. Place two pins on the sides of the basket handles to mark their positions. Remove the fabric

VEGGIE LUNCH TOTE

CONTINUED

from the basket, and cut
between the double pins
that mark the position of the
basket handles. Staying just
inside the marking pins, cut
a 4-inch-deep (10.2 cm) U
shape from each side of the
liner, as shown in figure 1.

3. Sew the fabric together using a ½-inch (1.3
cm) seam allowance. Stitch the bottom of the U,
leaving the sides of the U open. Stitch the sides
all the way around, leaving a 4-inch (10.2 cm)
section open for turning. Turn the fabric right
side out, and press. Whipstitch the opening
closed. Using a seam gauge, sew a pocket
around the entire liner, for the ties to slide
through, that is 2 inches (5.1 cm) in from the
outside edge of the basket.

4. Attach a safety pin onto
one tie and thread through
the pocket on one side, leaving the ends loose on either
side at the openings in the U.
Remove the safety pin, and
repeat with the other tie.

5. Place the liner in the bas-
ket, and tie the sashes into loose bows. Adjust
the liner so its gathers are evenly arranged
around the edge.

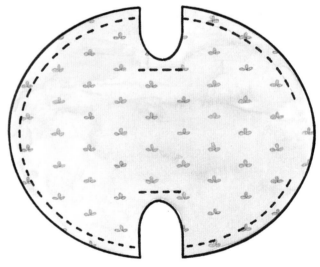

Fig. 1

Teddy Bear Toy Holder

DESIGNER: JEAN TOMASO MOORE

Jean Tomaso Moore's fanciful treatment brings these playful bears to life. One large bear hugs the toy basket, while his little friends cavort around the rim. The découpaged bear pictures came from a flea-market shirt.

Teddy Bear Toy Holder

CONTINUED

WHAT YOU'LL NEED

Bushel basket

Red acrylic spray paint

Checkerboard stencil, 2½ x 3½ inches
(6.4 x 8.9 cm)

Blue acrylic craft paint, 2-ounce (56 g) size

Stencil brush

Painter's tape

Wax paper for palette

Scissors

16 teddy bear images, 3 x 4 inches (7.6 x 10.2 cm)
each, cut from a piece of printed fabric, to fit
the size of basket's slats

Foam paintbrush

Acrylic découpage medium, glossy

1 yard (.9 m) blue-sky fabric, for lining (the pattern
used here came from a twin bed–size sheet)

Glue gun with glue sticks

2½ yards (2.3 m) red mini–polka dot grosgrain
ribbon, 1½ inches (3.8 cm) wide

3½ yards (3.2 m) white polka dot fabric ribbon,
¾ inch (1.9 cm) wide

½ yard (.45 m) sheer wired red-and-white-gingham
ribbon, 2 inches (5 cm) wide

Stuffed teddy bear, 18 inches (45.7 cm) tall

5 tiny stuffed, jointed teddy bears, each 3 inches
(7.6 cm) tall

INSTRUCTIONS

1. Spray paint the basket red. Allow to dry.

2. Stencil the checkerboard pattern in blue paint, onto every other slat of the basket. Use the painter's tape to hold the stencil in place as you go. Place a small amount of paint onto a palette made from wax paper. Dip the brush into the paint, then off-load the brush onto wax paper. Pounce the almost-dry brush onto the stencil.

3. Cut the bear motifs from the fabric; use these images to fill in the alternate spaces between the painted checkerboard pattern. Using the foam brush, apply découpage medium to the back of a cutout. Place the cutout onto the basket slat and smooth it down with your fingers. Apply another coat of découpage over the cutout. Apply all the bear images in this manner.

4. After all the bear cutouts are applied and dry, apply a final coat of découpage medium to the entire outside of the basket surface, to seal and protect it.

5. Drape the large square of lining fabric inside the basket. Use a bead of hot glue around the top rim of the basket to adhere the fabric, turning the raw edge under as you press it into place. This gives a clean line at the top of the basket and will cover any rough basket material that might cause splinters.

6. Glue the 1½-inch-wide (3.8 cm) polka dot ribbon to the outside band at the top of the basket. Next, glue the ¾-inch-wide (1.9 cm) ribbon to the two other horizontal bands on the basket.

7. Use the wider polka dot ribbon to pad the handles. Wrap the ribbon around the entire handle, and glue the end into place to secure the wrap.

8. Tie a bow around the large bear's neck, using the sheer red-and-white gingham ribbon. See Bow Tying 101 on pages 12–13 for more about bows.

9. Place the basket on a level surface. Stand the bear against the basket, and find the best position to stabilize and balance the bear's body against the basket. Prop one of the bear's arms on the basket rim and one to the side, as if she's holding onto the basket. Hot glue the paws into place. Glue the bear's foot where it touches the base of the basket.

10. Adhere the five tiny bears in various sitting and hanging-on positions on the basket's rim (one was adhered to the large bear's shoulder; see detail photo).

PRECIOUS METALS CANDY BASKET

DESIGNER: ALLISON SMITH

Here's a dainty basket that's small enough to perch anywhere in the home. Gleaming metallic finishes cleverly transform this split-bamboo basket, and the oversized bows give the traditional shape more presence.

WHAT YOU'LL NEED

Small basket with wide brim and handle

Silver craft paint

Foam paintbrush

Gold craft paint

#6 round paintbrush

3 yards (2.7 m) wide silver mesh ribbon

Floral wire

Wire cutters

INSTRUCTIONS

1. Paint the basket silver. When painting the first coat, dilute the paint with an equal amount of water. Load the brush heavily with paint so it seeps into the cracks. Use undiluted paint for the second coat.

2. Paint the polka dots in gold with the round brush.

3. Make two triple-loop shoelace bows from the mesh ribbon. To make the bow, cut one 18-inch (45.7 cm) piece and one 12-inch (30.5 cm) piece of the ribbon. Loop the 18-inch (45.7 cm) piece back and forth to form three complete loops on each side. Tie the loops in the center using a 6-inch (15.2 cm) piece of wire, twisting to secure it. Cover the wire with the 12-inch (30.5 cm) piece of ribbon, wrapping the ribbon around the bow, tying it in the back, and leaving the ends loose to form the bow's streamers. Fan out and shape the ribbon; trim the ends. Secure the bows at the base of each handle with the wire.

VARIATION

Instead of silver mesh ribbon, add matte-finished mini-ornament clusters in deep jewel tones to the bases of the handle.

TO MARKET, TO MARKET

DESIGNER: TERRY TAYLOR

*Fill the basket with overflow harvest from your garden, then embellish
it with miniature produce to match. The tiny baskets make this
project a clever visual pun.*

WHAT YOU'LL NEED

Market basket (the example shown is
   14 inches [35.6 cm] long)

1 yard (.9 m) ribbon, ¾ inch (1.9 cm) wide

Miniature market baskets, you'll need at least 2

Miniature artificial fruit or vegetables

Scissors

Glue gun with glue sticks

Raffia

INSTRUCTIONS

1. Wrap the ribbon around the rim of the basket.
Trim the length with scissors.

2. Glue the ribbon to the basket rim. Start and
end the ribbon at the handle. You'll disguise the
seam with a small basket.

3. Glue the artificial fruit or vegetables into the
miniature baskets. Set them aside.

4. Tie three or four strands of raffia tightly to the
base of each handle with a simple overhand knot.

5. Glue a miniature basket to the handles on top
of the raffia. Trim the raffia as desired.

VARIATION

Mini-ribbon and artificial fruit and vegetables
come in all colors…use whatever strikes
your fancy!

FROSTED BEAD
HANGING BASKET

DESIGNER: TERRY TAYLOR

*This fabulous indoor/outdoor design is simple and modern. Be sure to
choose beads that are in proportion to the size of your basket.*

WHAT YOU'LL NEED

Metal hanging basket

14-gauge galvanized wire

Wire cutters

Parallel pliers

Large glass beads

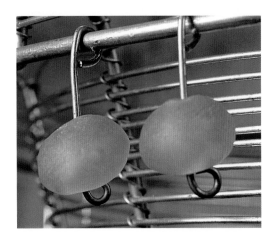

INSTRUCTIONS

1. Cut the wire into 5-inch (12.7 cm) lengths,
one for each bead you plan to hang on the basket.

2. Use the parallel pliers to make a C-shaped loop
at the top of each piece of wire.

3. Put a bead onto the other end of the wire.

4. Use the pliers to make a loop at the bottom of
the bead to hold it in place.

5. Hang the wire on the rim or bottom of the basket. Close the C-shaped loop so that the wire
stays in place on the basket.

6. Hang the rest of the beads on the wire basket,
following steps 2 through 5.

Willow Flatware Holder

DESIGNER: TERRY TAYLOR

Mismatched pieces of silverplate flatware decorate—and create the handles—on this willow cutlery basket. Use the basket to gather compliments and store your flatware at your next picnic or tailgate party.

WHAT YOU'LL NEED

- Willow cutlery basket
- 6 to 8 pieces silverplate flatware
- Electric drill and 3 mm drill bit
- Rolling pin
- Rubber or rawhide mallet (optional)
- 24-gauge steel wire
- Wire cutters
- Flat-nose jewelry pliers

INSTRUCTIONS

1. Acquire your flatware by shopping at thrift stores, yard sales, or antique shops. You're sure to find a basket or box of mismatched, badly tarnished silverplate, inexpensively priced.

2. Use the electric drill and the drill bit to drill a pair of holes, spaced about ¼ inch (6 mm) apart, at the end of the handle and also on the bowl or tine end of each piece of flatware.

3. Choose two pieces to use as handles. Place the utensil on the rolling pin, and use considerable hand pressure to bend the piece to a slightly curved shape. If needed,

pound with the mallet to the desired shape. Check the shape by placing the utensil on the basket. When you're satisfied with the shape of the handle, repeat with a second utensil.

4. Cut several 8-inch (20.3 cm) lengths of the 24-gauge wire with the wire cutters. Set them aside.

5. Bend a length of wire in half. Thread the two ends through a pair of the holes you drilled in a handle piece. Weave and cross the wires around the willow weavers and stakes that give the basket its support and shape. For the best results, use the pliers to pull the wires rather than using your fingers. Tightly twist the two ends together, and use the wire cutters to closely snip the twisted wire. Tuck the twisted end into the willow. Repeat for the opposite end of the utensil.

6. Attach the second handle as you did in the previous step.

7. Embellish the sides of the basket with the other utensils in the same way.

HOME UTILITY TOTE

DESIGNER: CORINNE KURZMANN

What could be more functional than a plastic basket with a hardworking chrome handle? Use it to carry fix-it tools or cleaning supplies anywhere in the house or garden.

WHAT YOU'LL NEED

Plastic basket with holes and chrome handle

Grommets with ¼-inch-diameter (6 mm) opening

Grommet setting tool

Selection of washers, available at hardware and
home improvement stores

INSTRUCTIONS

1. Embellish a pattern of holes in the basket with grommets. Follow the manufacturer's recommendations for using the grommet setting tool.

2. Remove the handle from the basket, and thread two different-sized washers onto each end, then replace the handle.

VARIATION

Purchase brightly colored hair ornaments at a discount store. If they're attached to bobby pins or barrettes, they'll snap off easily. Adhere them to your utility basket with hot glue, and go!

Handmade Paper Découpaged Basket

DESIGNER: JEAN TOMASO MOORE

Turn an ordinary gift fruit basket into a work of modern sculpture! Designer Jean Tomaso Moore added twig legs to this basket's clean shape, for a surprisingly sophisticated look.

Wicker fruit basket

2 sheets handmade paper, each 20 x 30 inches
(50.8 x 76.2 cm): 1 white sheet with colored
confetti specks and 1 ecru sheet with embedded
bark and leaves

Acrylic découpage medium, matte finish

Stiff-bristled paintbrush

4 pieces of tree branch, each 5 inches (12.7 cm) long

Handsaw or optional miter box

Electric drill with a drill bit diameter several times
larger than the 22-gauge wire

22-gauge colored or copper wire, 2 yards (1.8 m) long

Wire cutter

Glue gun with glue sticks

Electric palm sander (optional)

INSTRUCTIONS

1. Protect your work surface, or work in an area
where splashes of water won't do any damage. Rip
the two sheets of handmade paper into large,
irregular pieces.

2. Use the découpage medium, heavily diluted
with water, to attach the torn pieces of paper to
the basket. Brush the medium onto the basket,
lay a piece of paper onto it, then brush over the
top of the paper, saturating it with the solution.
Use the stiff-bristled brush to work the paper into
the weave of the basket. Add all the pieces of
paper in this manner, overlapping them as you go,
until the entire basket is covered. Allow 24 hours
for the basket to thoroughly dry.

3. To make the legs, cut four branches of similar
thickness into 5-inch (12.7 cm) lengths. Use a
miter box if you wish to make even, accurate cuts.

4. Snug one of the legs against the inside of the
rim on the basket's base. Drill two small holes,
one above the other, ½ inch (1.3 cm) apart,
through both the rim and the leg. Repeat the
drilling for the other three legs.

5. Cut four 18-inch (45.7 cm) pieces of wire. To
attach the leg to the basket, thread a piece of wire
several times through the holes you drilled. Bring
the ends of the wire to the inside, twist them
securely together, and snip the ends. Repeat for
the other three legs. Hot-glue the legs where they
touch the inside of the rim.

6. Stand the basket on its legs. Check it with a
level, using a sanding tool if you need to even the
legs a bit more.

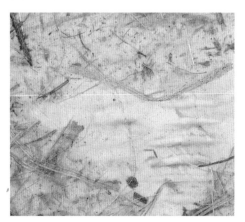

Jingle Bells

DESIGNER: JEAN TOMASO MOORE

You'll make a merry tune as o'er the fields you go, laughing all the way. The red-velvet liner gives this basket a fancy touch.

5-inch-square (12.7 cm) flat weave reed basket
with handle

Metallic gold latex acrylic spray paint

135 gold bells, 16 mm in diameter

7 yards (6.3 m) 24-gauge gold beading wire

Wire cutters

1 yard (.9 m) red and gold metallic ribbon,
⅜ inch (9.5 mm) wide

Scissors

Glue gun with glue sticks

Red velvet, 10 x 10 inches (25.4 x 25.4 cm)

10 to 12 red bells, 9 mm in diameter

½ yard (.45 m) red satin ribbon, ⅛ inch
(3 mm) wide

1 red bell, 16 mm in diameter

1 green bell, 16 mm in diameter

1 large gold bell, 1 inch (2.5 cm) in diameter

INSTRUCTIONS

1. Spray paint the basket gold. Allow it to dry.

2. Using wire cutters, cut 27 pieces of wire, each
9 inches (22.9 cm) long.

3. Thread five 16-mm gold bells onto each wire.
From the outside of the basket, push the ends
of the wired bells through the spaces in the basket's weave. Twist the two ends of the wire
inside the basket to secure the bells. Wire all
the bells closely together around the entire rim
of the basket.

4. Cut a length of the red and gold metallic ribbon equal to the basket's circumference, weaving
the ribbon through a reed in the middle of the
basket's side. Overlap the ends of the ribbon on
the inside of the bas-
ket, using a dab of
hot glue to hold
them in place. Weave
a piece of the ribbon
into the handle.

5. Use the square of
red velvet fabric to
hide the exposed
wires inside the bas-
ket. Drape the fabric
inside the basket.
Turn the raw edges under, and use hot glue
around the inner rim to hold the fabric in place.

6. Thread the 9-mm red bells onto the ⅛-inch-
wide (3 mm) red satin ribbon, knotting the ribbon between each bell. Drape these bells over the
handle and tie them into place.

7. Thread the red and green 16-mm bells and the
large 1-inch (2.5 cm) gold bell onto a length of
the narrow red ribbon, and tie this ribbon around
the small bells.

Glass Dangles Wire Pedestal

DESIGNER: ALLISON SMITH

This modern pedestal-style wire basket is the perfect way to show off simple glass bead pendants in warm reds and golds. This is such a quick and easy method, you can change the look for a special occasion.

What You'll Need

Black round wire basket (in the example, the basket has 8 ribs)

48 glass seed beads

8 brass spacers

8 round handblown glass beads

8 cylindrical glass beads

8 coin-shaped beads

8 glass teardrop beads

18-gauge black wire

Needle-nose pliers

Round-nosed jewelry pliers

Wire cutters

Instructions

1. Determine how many beaded embellishments you would like to hang on your basket. Some wire baskets are vertically divided by the ribs into sections; as a general guideline, hang one beaded embellishment per section.

2. For each section you'll need one large round handblown glass bead, one cylindrical glass bead, one coin-shaped glass bead, one small teardrop bead, one small brass spacer, and six seed beads. Keep the beads in the same color family. It might be nice to choose a color that will coordinate with your room décor.

3. For every beaded embellishment, cut one 6-inch (15.2 cm) piece of black wire. To keep the beads on the wire, make a small, tight coil at the end of each one. Lace the beads onto the wire in this order: one seed bead, the brass spacer, the large round glass bead, two seed beads, the cylindrical bead, two seed beads, the coin-shaped bead, the teardrop-shaped bead, and one seed bead.

4. To attach the embellishment, bend the wire with the pliers, wrapping the end of the wire around the edge of the basket. You'll have plenty of extra wire to work with, but keep the top of the last bead close to the edge of the basket. Wrap the wire around the edge three times, then wrap the wire around itself once and cut off the excess.

5. Repeat the process for the remaining beaded embellishments.

Wintry Carryall

DESIGNER: JEAN TOMASO MOORE

*Frosty floral stems bedeck this oversized basket, and the limited color palette suggests
a chilly winter's day. Let it hold a season's worth of hard apples, or use it to serve
napkin-wrapped silverware at a fancy winter buffet.*

What You'll Need

Large basket with handle (this one came painted
   a glossy forest green)

2 artificial white berry stems, 30 inches (76.2 cm)
   in length

22-gauge green florist's wire

Wire cutters

2 thin twig branches, painted white, 30 inches
   (76.2 cm) in length

2 artificial white flocked floral clusters with green leaves

1 stem with green leaves and white frosted ½-inch
   (1.3 cm) ball ornaments

2 artificial purple flocked floral clusters with green leaves

1 pine cone

Artificial snow (aerosol)

Glue gun with glue stick

Instructions

1. Lay one of the long
stems of white berries
over the handle, keeping
the stem end in the center
of the handle and letting
the ends drape around the handle. Use green
florist's wire to attach the stem to the handle.
Overlap the second berry stem onto the first one,
facing it in the opposite direction to create a sym-
metrical balance. Wire this stem to the handle.

2. Add a twig branch to each side of the arrangement, overlapping them at the center. Wrap them
securely with wire.

3. Add a stem of the flocked white flowers to each
side of the arrangement, once again securing them
with florist's wire.

4. Position the stem with the ball ornament, then
bend it so that it clings to one side of the arrangement. Wire it to the handle.

5. Bend some of the leaves from the flowers over
the wire elements to hide the wire.

6. Place one of the purple flocked stems opposite
the larger frosted ball stem. Wire it on.

7. To fill out the arrangement, cut off small pieces
of the other purple stem and hot glue them into
any bare spots.

8. Spray the pine cone with the aerosol "snow."
Use the glue gun to adhere the pine cone onto
the top of the handle as an added textural element. If needed, bend more of the leaves around
exposed wires to hide them.

WOODBURNED BASKET

DESIGNER: SUSAN KIEFFER

Keep this basket handy when you're gathering herbs from the garden.
Designer Susan Kieffer applied a simple geometric motif to a
split-wood market basket.

WHAT YOU'LL NEED

- Small market basket
- Golden oak wood stain
- Colonial pine wood stain
- Foam paintbrushes
- Woodburning or branding kit with diamond, script, and all-purpose points
- Decorative elastic
- Sewing needle and coordinating thread

INSTRUCTIONS

1. Paint the entire basket, inside and out, with golden oak wood stain. Let dry, then stain it again. Let dry.

2. Use the colonial pine wood stain to paint all the left-to-right diagonal strips, the band on the rim (inside and out), and both sides of the handle. Let dry.

3. Screw the diamond design into the tool, and preheat it for approximately eight minutes (or follow the manufacturer's directions for preheating). Hold the tool perpendicular to the surface while working, and burn the diamond shape onto the center of each right-to-left diagonal strip and also onto the handle. It takes only two or three seconds to make each mark.

4. Place the tool in its holder; unplug it, and let it cool, then insert the script point. Make little lines close together on the edges of all the strips around the basket. Then, using the all-purpose point, which creates a straight line, continue adding to the diamond sections by burning lines on each side of the diamond and at two of the diamond points.

5. On each of the left-to-right diagonal strips, create another design using the all-purpose point.

6. Cut the decorative elastic about 1 inch (2.5 cm) shorter than the perimeter of the basket's band. Sew the elastic ends together, and slide it onto the band.

Moss-Lined Planter

DESIGNER: SUSAN KIEFFER

Since the moss that lines this basket needs daily misting, you might consider planting the basket for a special occasion, and then return the plant back to its regular pot. Using a bromeliad gives this beautiful design a tropical flavor.

WHAT YOU'LL NEED

Wire basket with ½ to 1-inch (1.3 to 2.5 cm) spaces in the weave

Package of live green sheet moss

Plant mister or spray bottle

Plastic bag

Moisture-loving plant (pictured here is a "Vella" *Guzmania* bromeliad)

Spanish moss

INSTRUCTIONS

Note: It's best to water only the bottom cups of a bromeliad; be careful not to overfill them. Ferns are another good choice for a moist, mossy environment. If live green sheet moss is not available in your area, you can substitute the dried grayish sheet moss. Floral designers often use this and spray paint the moss a grass-green color. If you use dry moss, water only the plant, not the moss.

1. Mist the live sheet moss to make sure it's moist and pliable. Using pieces as tall as the basket, press the moss firmly against the basket, with the green side facing to the outside, until it pokes through the openings. Continue pressing and poking moss until all the openings are filled.

2. Place an open plastic bag on the bottom of the basket, and nestle it against the moss. Put a small potted plant in the bag.

3. Tuck the Spanish moss under the plant leaves, and spread it to cover the edges of the pot and the plastic bag. Mist daily to keep the moss green and the plant healthy.

VARIATION

Adhere (or hang) little ceramic embellishments, such as these lively garden visitors, onto the sides of the basket.

FEATHERED EASTER BASKET

DESIGNER: JEAN TOMASO MOORE

When you're ready to hide—or find—the Easter eggs,
this feathery beauty is just right.

WHAT YOU'LL NEED

    Oval basket with handles

    Acrylic spray paint (mint green or other
        pastel color)

    2 bags of pastel colored craft feathers, .25 ounce
        (7 g)

    Glue gun with glue sticks

    1 dozen plastic eggs, 2 inches (5 cm) long

    Sandpaper

    Acrylic craft paints in pastel shades of peach,
        yellow, pink, lavender, and blue, 2 ounces
        (56 g) each

    Paintbrush

INSTRUCTIONS

1. Spray paint the basket mint green.

2. Hot-glue the feathers all over the wicker basket. Poke the feathers into the openings in the basket's weave.

3. Rough up the plastic eggs with sandpaper so the paint will stick to them, then paint the eggs with various shades of the craft paints.

4. Glue several eggs to the outside and the rim of the basket.

VARIATION

Change the mood—and the seasonal flavor—by using tinsel and other holiday-motif embellishments.

Celestial Celebration

DESIGNER: CORINNE KURZMANN

Playful star shapes combine with elegant gold wire to make this wire basket a celebration in itself. The perfect gift basket for a New Year's party, housewarming, birthday, or any joyous occasion.

WHAT YOU'LL NEED

Gold star-shaped basket

2 sheets gold tissue paper

2 sheets white tissue paper printed with gold stars

Star-shaped cookie cutter

Sharp pencil

Scissors

Powdered découpage medium

Small container with lid

Small foam paintbrush

Wet rag

INSTRUCTIONS

1. Make eight star shapes by tracing the outline of the cookie cutter on the back of the gold tissue paper. Trace 17 star shapes on the decorated white tissue paper.

2. Carefully cut the star shapes from the tissue paper.

3. Mix the découpage powder with water in a small container until it reaches a paste consistency.

4. Use the small paintbrush to apply the découpage paste to the back of each star, then press them against the basket. Overlap the stars and alternate their colors as you work your way around the basket. Keep a wet rag within reach to wipe your hands as they become sticky.

5. Once all of the stars are in place, smooth a thin layer of the découpage paste over the fronts of the stars. The paste will appear white when you apply it, but it will dry to a clear finish.

6. Cover the découpage paste and set it aside. When the first coat of paste has dried, reapply a second layer and let it dry.

7. Cut the remaining tissue paper into narrow strips, to use as decorative fill.

CHINESE COINS

DESIGNER: CORINNE KURZMANN

Unusual Chinese coins emphasize this basket's Oriental appearance. The sturdy basket design and rich coloring make it an excellent choice to hold heavier items, or you can line it with plastic to hold a fern.

WHAT YOU'LL NEED

Large Chinese basket (8½ x 11 inches [21.6 x 27.9 cm] at the rim)

1 large and two small antique Chinese coins (available at bead stores)

1 yard (.9 m) lightweight black upholstery cord

1 medium and 2 small red glass beads with large center holes

Scissors

Sewing needle and thread coordinated to the glass bead color (optional)

2 small black tassels

2 medium black tassels

2 scarab beads with large center holes

2 yards (1.8 m) lightweight black upholstery cord (to match the tassels)

1 yard (.9 m) medium-weight black upholstery cord (to match the tassels)

Glue gun with glue sticks

Tape

INSTRUCTIONS

1. To secure the large coin in the center of one side of the basket, first, from the inside, pull both ends of the lightweight cord through the center of the basket, to the outside. Then, wrap the cord around and through the coin and the larger glass bead, as shown in the photo. If you can't fit the cord through the bead, sew it onto the cord at the center of the coin with a needle and thread. Continue using the ends of the cord to attach the smaller coins on either side of the larger one, so that all the coins are held by one piece of cord. The basket's weave should be tight enough to keep the cord from slipping, but if it isn't, knot the cord (on the inside of the basket) behind each coin. Leave the cords several inches long on the inside of the basket.

CHINESE COINS

CONTINUED

2. Make the embellishments that hang below the smaller coins. Thread the hanging loop from a smaller tassel with a scarab bead and a glass bead. Pull the tassel's loop through the basket weave and knot it on

3. Tape the ends of the cord to keep them from unraveling.

4. Cut two pieces of the medium-weight cord that are equal to one-half of the rim's circumference *plus 1 inch (2.5 cm)*. Hot-glue this cord

the other side. If it isn't long enough, pull a short loop of the lightweight cord through the weave, directly under a smaller coin, leaving the tail on the inside of the basket. Stitch through the small bead to attach it to the loop. Pull or knot the cord from the inside of the basket, so the embellishment lies snugly against the basket's side.

in place around the rim of the basket, with the ends meeting up on the shorter sides of the basket. Knot the ends of the cord on each side of the basket, and fray the ends.

5. Hot-glue a larger tassel by its loop, where the ends of the cords meet, on each side of the basket.

FAIRY TOTE

DESIGNER: CORINNE KURZMANN

All manner of fairies use this basket to sprinkle moonbeams and stardust hither and yon. You, too, can carry a special gift in it to your favorite sprite. The clever fabric collar nearly doubles the capacity of this charming basket.

FAIRY TOTE

CONTINUED

WHAT YOU'LL NEED

Basket with tall handle

Measuring tape

Scissors

¼ yard (.23 m) coordinating "fairy print" fabric
for the collar and collar lining (in the
example, the same green-and-purple printed
cotton was used for both)

Aerosol basting spray

Sewing machine

Straight pins

Iron

Sewing needle and coordinating thread

5 frosted-plastic buttons

Large safety pin

9 yards (8.1 m) of purple ribbon,
1 inch (2.5 cm) wide

Fairy figurine

INSTRUCTIONS

1. Measure the circumference of the basket.
Double this measurement and add 2 inches (5.1
cm) for the seams. Measure the vertical part of the
basket, adding 4 inches (10.2 cm) to this measurement, for the drawstrings. Cut one piece each
of outer and lining fabrics to these dimensions.

2. Spray the wrong sides of the fabric pieces with
the basting spray, following the manufacturer's
directions. Turn the fabric's raw edges in.

3. Layer the two pieces of fabric with their right
sides out, and press them together.

4. With the lining side out, pin and sew the two
short sides together, but only halfway across. To
make an opening for the basket
handle, clip into the seam
allowance at the halfway point,
then iron the seam open. Pin
the raw edges of the opening,
as shown in figure 1.

5. To make the opening for the
other end of the handle, cut
the collar in half vertically on
the side opposite the seam; see figure 2. Finish
these raw edges.

76

6. Now make the drawstring channels. Turn in and pin ¼ inch (6 mm) of the long sides' raw edges to the lining side. Sew closely along the edges. Turn and pin the edges of the long sides under 1¼ inches (3.2 cm), to the lining side. Sew both channels closed with a double line of stitching. As you sew, turn the stitching at the corners, to finish the edges of the opening you made in step 4.

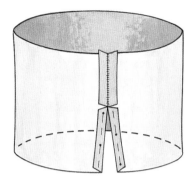

Fig. 1

7. Attach a safety pin to one end of the purple ribbon, and thread it through the drawstring opening.

8. Tack the two sides of the collar openings closed around each end of the handle; use a button at the back opening, for added embellishment.

9. Tie the drawstrings into bows, securing the bottom of the collar snugly around and just below the basket's rim.

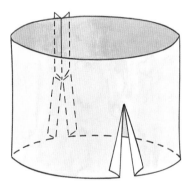

Fig. 2

10. Wrap the handle with ribbon. Cut a separate length of ribbon, and tie a shoelace bow to hide the end of the wrapping on the handle. For more information, see Bow-Tying 101 on page 12. Sew buttons onto the ends of each of the drawstring ribbons.

11. Tie a thread onto the figurine, and attach her to the handle.

POTTERY SHARD MOSAIC

DESIGNER: TERRY TAYLOR

Don't throw away that beloved broken Italian or Portuguese platter. Use the brightly glazed shards to decorate the broad rim of a rustic basket with them.

WHAT YOU'LL NEED

Basket with broad wooden rim

Pottery shards

Tile nippers

Rock tumbler with coarse grinding grit

Kitchen towel

Glue gun and glue sticks

INSTRUCTIONS

1. Use the tile nippers to break the large shards into smaller-sized pieces. Keep in mind that the shards should be an appropriate size for the wooden rim of the basket.

2. Fill the barrel of the tumbler with the small shards and grinding grit, according to the manufacturer's instructions. Add the recommended amount of water, seal the barrel, and tumble the shards for at least 12 hours. When the tumbling time is finished, open the barrel and check that the sharp edges have been sufficiently rounded. If needed, tumble the shards for an additional 8 hours.

3. Remove the tumbled shards from the barrel. Rinse them well, and spread them out on a clean kitchen towel to dry.

4. Glue the shards to the top and sides of the wooden rim. Fit them closely together but not touching.

VARIATION

An eye-catching version uses tumbled beach glass or pretty rocks.

Woven Ribbon & Beads

DESIGNER: CORINNE KURZMANN

Alternating weaves of shimmering ribbon soften the bold lines of this chrome basket, while carefully placed beads enhance their light-reflective qualities—a simple technique with dazzling effects.

WHAT YOU'LL NEED

Wire basket with vertical ribs (this one measures
  9 x 11 inches [22.9 x 27.9 cm] at the rim)
60 purple glass beads with large holes
6 yards (5.4 m) sheer gray ribbon, 1½ inches
  (3.8 cm) wide
6 yards (5.4 m) sheer purple ribbon, 1½ inches
  (3.8 cm) wide
Scissors
Straight pins
Sewing needle
Silver or gray thread

INSTRUCTIONS

1. Thread five beads onto the gray ribbon. You'll space them out later.

2. Weave the beaded ribbon around the basket, over and under its ribs, until both ends meet. Cut off the excess ribbon, leaving 1 inch (2.5 cm) of it for the seam. Neatly fold the ends of the ribbon under, and pin them together with a straight pin.

3. Repeat these steps with the remaining ribbon, alternating the purple with the gray, until the entire basket is covered.

4. Sew the pinned ends of each of the ribbons together with needle and thread, working from the inside and starting at the bottom. Knot the end of the thread.

5. Slide the beads into position around the basket so they're evenly spaced.

Folk Art Hallowe'en Carryall

DESIGNER: ALLISON SMITH

Greet visiting ghosties and ghoulies with this fun treat carryall. A loosely woven rattan basket makes it a snap to attach folksy embellishments onto it.

What You'll Need

Medium-size basket with handle

Burlap, 18 x 36 inches (45.7 cm x .9 m)

Scissors

Glue gun

Black mini rickrack trim, 18 inches (45.7 cm) in length (found at fabric stores)

Embroidery needle

Black thread

Black paper ribbon

18-gauge black wire

Wire cutters

Two large orange buttons

Yellow and orange felt, 1 sheet of each

Black felt, 2 sheets

Orange, yellow, black, red, and purple embroidery floss

Cotton balls

Green paper ribbon

Four large black buttons

Instructions

1. Place the unfolded burlap in the bottom of the basket, carefully smoothing and tucking it to create a lining for the basket. Trim the edges of the burlap, leaving 1 inch (2.5 cm) extra around the edges. Fold the raw edges under and tack the lining in place with the glue gun. Whipstitch the rickrack to the folded edge of the burlap.

2. Make two double-loop shoelace bows from 18-inch (45.7 cm) pieces of the black paper ribbon. Tie the pairs of loops together in the center by twisting them with a 6-inch (15.2 cm) piece of wire. Cover the wire with a 12-inch (30.5 cm) piece of ribbon, wrapping it around the bow. Tie the ribbon in the back, leaving the ends loose to make the bow's streamers. Fan out and shape the ribbon, trimming the ends into a deep zigzag. Glue one orange button onto the center of each ribbon. Secure the bows onto the ends of the basket with the wire.

Folk Art Hallowe'en Basket

CONTINUED

3. Using the patterns provided (see figure 1), trace and cut out four crescent moons in yellow felt, four pumpkins in orange felt, and eight cats in black felt. Using three strands of orange floss, create a stuffed moon by sewing two of the felt pieces together with a blanket stitch, as shown in figure 2. Leave a small opening. Stuff the moon with three cotton balls, then finish stitching. Repeat with the other moon pieces.

For the pumpkins, stitch four black curved lines with three strands of embroidery floss onto two of the pumpkin cutouts. Whipstitch an embroi-

dered front onto a plain pumpkin back, stuffing it with five or six cotton balls before finishing off the seam. Repeat with the other pumpkin cutouts. Embellish the pumpkins with a 1-inch (2.5 cm) piece of green paper ribbon. Leave it twisted at the top, and untwist the bottom half to form the stem. Attach them to the pumpkins with a dab of hot glue.

For the cats, embroider faces onto four of the cat cutouts. Make little yellow French knots (figure 3) for the eyes, and use red satin stitches (figure 4) to make a little triangle

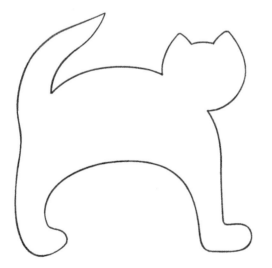

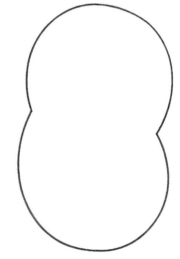

Fig. 1

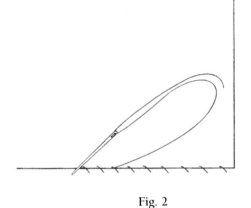

Fig. 2

nose and a mouth. Make sure to embroider the cat faces so that they will be facing each other when positioned on the basket. Whipstitch the embroidered fronts onto the plain cat backs using the purple embroidery floss. Stuff the cats with cotton balls before stitching them closed.

4. Cut two pieces of wire that are twice as long as the basket. Using the pliers, make groups of small twists and coils in the wire to simulate grapevines. The wire should be the length of the basket when you are finished. Hot-glue two cats, one moon, and two black buttons onto each piece of wire with a dab of hot glue. Then, attach the entire assembly onto the side of the basket with more hot glue. Lastly, hot-glue the pumpkin onto the lower half of the basket using still more hot glue. Repeat for the other side of the basket.

Fig. 4

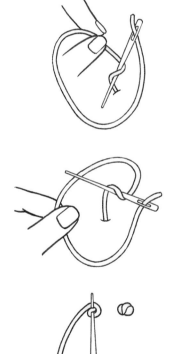

Fig. 3

Gilded Basket

DESIGNER: JANE LA FERLA

Gather compliments when you turn an ordinary basket into a gleaming, glowing accent for the home. The stunning, variegated copper leaf treatment by designer Jane La Ferla brings a mellow finish to this lovely basket.

What You'll Need

Basket, unfinished or painted

Clear shellac

Two 2-inch (5 cm) disposable foam brushes

Water-based size

Copper leaf (review gilding instructions
    on page 18)

Tissue paper (optional)

Green variegated leaf

2-inch (5 cm) bristle brush (optional)

Acrylic varnish

Instructions

1. Seal the basket with clear shellac, or use a painted or whitewashed one that's already sealed.

2. Apply the size to the inside of the basket, and dry it to the tack stage. The size should coat only the exterior surfaces of the ribs or stakes, allowing the leaf to highlight the weaving. Don't try to cover all the ins and outs of the basket's surfaces.

3. Following the manufacturer's instructions for the leaf product you're using, begin applying the leaf tissue in the bottom of the basket, and work up the sides. For some types of leaf, it may be necessary to press the material into place with tissue paper, rather than with your fingers, and to remove any excess leaf with a bristle brush.

4. Apply size to the outside of the basket, and when it reaches the tack stage of drying, repeat step 3.

5. Apply size randomly on outer areas of the basket. When the size becomes tacky, apply smaller pieces of variegated leaf to accent the copper leaf you applied first.

6. Finally, apply size to the handle. Cut smaller pieces of copper leaf for this area. Apply the leaf as before.

7. Let the leaf set for 24 hours, then use a foam brush to apply the gloss varnish. Begin with the inside of the basket and work to the outside.

Essential Catchall

DESIGNER: CORINNE KURZMANN

Here's an excellent catchall basket for art supplies, sewing implements, or stationery. A pretty piece of origami paper, held under glass in the basket's bottom, adds a personal touch.

What You'll Need

- Large serving basket with added-on wooden handles
- 6 yards (5.4 m) blue upholstery cord
- Tape
- 4 glass spacer beads with large center holes
- Scissors
- Pencil or skewer
- Origami paper, photo, or original artwork
- Sheet of single-strength glass cut to fit in the bottom of the basket (ask the glass shop to polish the edges)

Instructions

1. Cut the existing material that holds the handles in place, so you can remove them.

2. Cut the blue upholstery cord into four 1½-yard (1.35 m) pieces. Tape the ends, or melt them with a lighter, to prevent the threads from separating.

3. Slip a glass bead over one end of a section of the cord. Insert the cord's end through a hole in the handle, until a short length of it extends from the bottom of the handle. Slide the glass bead so that it sits on the top of the handle. Press the handle against the top of the basket, with the excess cord pinched between the two. Weave the remaining cord around the handle and through the basket, working from the end of the handle to the center. Hide the cord's end between the handle and the basket; use a pencil or skewer to push it out of sight. Repeat for the other ends of the handles.

4. Select an interesting paper or a picture to put in the bottom of the basket. Measure the inside bottom of the basket with a measuring tape and cut the paper to fit. If you have several smaller images, collage them together on a piece of light cardboard cut to fit. Cover the image with a piece of glass.

SPRING INTO SUMMER

DESIGNER: ALLISON SMITH

The updated color combination gives this deep-dyed basket an eyecatching designer look. Coloring baskets is fun and easy!

WHAT YOU'LL NEED

Unfinished small basket with handle

Canning pot large enough to hold your basket

Packet of purple dye powder

36 inches (.9 m) organza ribbon, 3 inches
    (7.6 cm) wide

Floral wire

Wire cutters

Scissors

Gossamer butterflies or dragonflies

INSTRUCTIONS

1. Fill the canning pot with 2 to 3 gallons (7.6 to 11.4 L) of water. Place on the stove over medium heat and add the purple dye. When the water starts to simmer, submerge the basket in the dye. Carefully turn the basket to cover all surfaces. Watch the basket, leaving it in the dye bath long enough for a nice, rich color to develop. The time necessary will vary due to differences between brands. Remove the basket and allow it to dry on a flattened garbage bag that has been covered with several sheets of newspaper.

2. Make two double-loop shoelace bows out of the organza ribbon (for more information, see Bow Tying 101). To make a bow, cut one 18-inch (45.7 cm) piece and one 12-inch (30.5 cm) piece of the ribbon. Loop the 18-inch (45.7 cm) piece back and forth to form three complete loops on each side. Tie the loops in the center using a 6-inch (15.2 cm) piece of wire, twisting it tightly to secure it. Cover the wire with the 12-inch (30.5 cm) piece of ribbon, wrapping the ribbon around

the bow, tying it in the back, and leaving the ends loose to create the bow's streamers. Fan out and shape the ribbon, then trim the ends. Secure the bows onto the ends of the basket with the wire.

3. Secure the gossamer butterflies onto the basket handle.

TOPIARY MAGAZINE HOLDER

DESIGNER: ALLISON SMITH

Elegant gold details and a formal topiary scene are featured in Allison Smith's design. This rattan basket, reinforced with wood strips, is sturdy enough to hold an entire collection of catalogs or magazines.

WHAT YOU'LL NEED

Wood and rattan rectangular basket

Foam paintbrush, 1 inch (2.5 cm) wide

2 foam paintbrushes, each 3 inches (7.6 cm) wide

Acrylic paint in gold, dark red, and champagne (pale gold)

#6 flat paint brush

Topiary-theme paper découpage decals (available in craft stores) or colorful design cut from strong paper

Découpage medium (optional)

Matte varnish

Sponge

2 tassels (optional)

INSTRUCTIONS

1. Using the 1-inch (2.5 cm) foam paintbrush, coat the rattan with the pale gold paint, making sure that all cracks get filled. While the paint is still wet, drag a *dry* 3-inch (7.6 cm) foam paintbrush across the rattan basket to remove any excess paint. Allow to dry.

2. Paint the wood with the gold paint, applying the paint in only one direction for each coat. While the second coat is still wet, create streaks by dragging a *dry* 3-inch (7.6 cm) brush through the paint.

3. Paint the insides edge of the wood with the dark red paint, using the #6 brush.

4. To apply the decals, wet and smooth them into the rattan with a wet sponge. As an alternative, adhere paper cutouts with découpage medium, following the manufacturer's directions. Allow to dry.

5. Paint over the rattan with two coats of matte varnish. If the basket has handles, tie tassels onto them.

Baby Doll Bed

DESIGNER: ALLISON SMITH

*Here's a great way to show off a lovely doll from your collection. For a luxurious look,
use generous amounts of fabric in coordinating mini-prints.*

WHAT YOU'LL NEED

Oval wicker laundry basket (in the example,
the basket measures 24 inches [61 cm]
long and 9 inches [22.9 cm] high)

$2\frac{2}{3}$ yards (2.4 m) cotton fabric with an allover
print for liner and skirt, 45 inches (1.1 m) wide;
see figure 1 for suggested cutting layout

Coordinating fabric in two different prints for
coverlet and pillow

Measuring tape

Scissors

Sewing machine

Thread

Straight pins

Quilt batting

Polyester stuffing

Embroidery floss in coordinating color

Embroidery needle

Lace

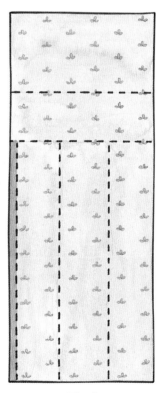

Fig. 1

INSTRUCTIONS

Note: You can save a lot of time by tearing, rather than cutting, the fabric. Just snip an edge, then tear—it always makes a straight line.

1. Measure the basket and lay out the pieces as efficiently as possible.

For the skirt: To find the total length, measure the circumference of the basket and multiply this number by 2.5; divide the total by 3. For the width, measure the height of the basket and add $1\frac{1}{2}$ inches (3.8 cm). Cut three pieces of fabric to these measurements.

For the liner: To find the length and width, use a measuring tape to measure the inside of the basket from edge to edge, down along the sides, and across the bottom. Cut one piece of fabric from these measurements.

For the cushion: Use the measuring tape to find the length and width of the basket halfway up the inside. Cut two pieces of fabric this size.

2. Sew the wrong sides of the three skirt pieces together, creating a large circle. Press the seams open. Along the top edge, make a gather by sewing a very large zigzag stitch over a piece of thread. Gently draw this loose thread in from both ends to create a ruffle. Set aside.

3. Place the liner fabric, right side up, inside the basket. Smooth and tuck it into place, keeping the fabric positioned so that the gathers lie evenly around the sides of the basket. Drape the excess material over the sides and trim it to a 3-inch (7.6 cm) overhang. Pin the gathers to keep them in position.

4. Place the skirt in the basket with the right side facing down and the ruffled edge lying along the top edge of the basket. Arrange the ruffles so they are even all the way around, pinning them to the liner at the outside of the basket's top edge. Sew along this line. Trim away any excess fabric, and press the seams open.

5. Put the liner back into the basket and pin around the hem line, trimming off any excess fabric. Sew a ½-inch (1.3 cm) hem around the skirt.

6. With the right sides facing, sew the edges of the cushion fabric together, leaving a 4-inch (10.2 cm) opening on a long side, for turning. Measure

4 inches (10.2 cm) in from each corner, and stitch a line across the corners, as shown in figure 2. Turn the fabric right side out and stuff with polyester filling. Whipstitch the opening closed.

7. For the pillow, cut two 7 x 9-inch (17.8 x 22.9 cm) pieces of the coordinating fabric. Sew the pieces with the right sides facing. Turn, stuff, and whipstitch the opening.

8. For the coverlet, cut two pieces of the coordinating fabric 24 x 24 inches (61 x 61 cm). Cut a piece of the quilt batting to the same size. Place the fabric with the right sides together on top of the quilt batting. Pin the lace, facing inward, along the outside edge of the fabric (between the two pieces of fabric). Sew, leaving 4 inches (10.2 cm) for turning. Trim the seams, then turn the fabric right side out, and press. Whipstitch the seam closed. Tack the three layers together with embroidery floss at 8-inch (20.3 cm) intervals.

Fig. 2

VARIATION
Make the pillow and the outer skirt with pieces cut from a Battenberg lace tablecloth or pillowcase (available at craft stores).

Seashore Pedestal

DESIGNER: TERRY TAYLOR

This beautiful and versatile footed basket is pretty enough to show off on a side table.
Here, designer Terry Taylor transformed it into a display for favorite seashells.

What You'll Need

Woven, footed basket

Selection of seashells

Glue gun with glue sticks

Instructions

1. Select your shells with an eye to their proportion relative to the basket you're using.

2. Adhere each shell with a dab of hot glue. Hold it in place for at least 20 seconds, or until the shell is firmly attached to the basket.

Variation

Try using silk autumn leaves for a seasonal adaptation.

Sunny Birdfeed Wall Hanging

DESIGNER: CORINNE KURZMAN

Designer Corinne Kurzmann turned this sunburst basket into a bright reminder of late summer.

WHAT YOU'LL NEED

Round, flat sunburst-design basket

Unsalted sunflower seeds, 1 cup (220 g)

Glue gun and glue sticks

Polyurethane spray

Silk sunflower

Floral wire

Wire cutters

INSTRUCTIONS

1. Hot-glue the sunflower seeds in a pattern on the bottom of the basket.

2. Spray the top of the basket with the polyurethane spray. Let it dry. Repeat for the underside.

3. Hot-glue the silk sunflower in the center of the basket's base.

4. Cut a short length of the floral wire. Pass one end through the back of the basket and fashion it into a small loop for hanging. Twist the ends of the wire securely.

VARIATION

Weave strands of black raffia through the open weave around the edge of the basket.

3 TIERS

DESIGNER: JEAN TOMASO MOORE

Wedding guests can pluck tiny bags of birdseed (or the wedding program) from this versatile hanging basket. Or simply hang it, filled with soaps, towels, and bath salts, near the bath.

WHAT YOU'LL NEED

3-tier basket joined with cords, or 3 stacking
    baskets with small handles

Light pink acrylic enamel spray paint (or a color
    that complements your décor)

Measuring tape or ruler

7 yards (6.3 m) wired grosgrain ribbon, ½ inch
    (1.3 cm) wide, in a checkered pattern
    (in the sample, pale pink, yellow, white,
    and peach were used)

Scissors

50 peach/pink silk daisies, 1½ inches (3.8 cm)
    in diameter

27 white silk daisies, 3 inches
    (7.6 cm) in diameter

Glue gun with glue sticks

Large tassel (optional)

INSTRUCTIONS

1. Spray paint the basket pink.

2. This basket originally had thick cords; leave these on until you replace them with ribbon. The two lower baskets are joined by short pieces of wired ribbon; cut six pieces of the ribbon to the same length as the original rope ties. Add the ribbon to the two bottom tiers, knotting all of the ends around the basket handles. Cut away the original ropes.

3. Use one long piece of ribbon between two of the handles on the top basket. Cut a second, shorter, piece of ribbon for the third handle. Create a hanging loop in the center of the longer length of ribbon by wrapping the loose end of the shorter one around it several times, as shown in figure 1. Dab a bit of hot glue to hold the wrapped end of the ribbon in place.

4. Glue pink daisies around the entire rim of the bottom basket. Also glue one pink daisy and three white ones to each handle over the knotted ribbon.

5. Glue four silk daisies to the underside of the hanging loop.

6. Add a large tassel to the underside of the bottom basket for additional embellishment, if desired, using hot glue to hold it in place.

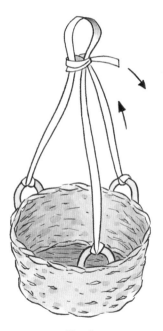

Fig. 1

VICTORIAN WIRE TRAY

DESIGNER: ALLISON SMITH

*The big, romantic silk gardenias on this low-profile wire basket bring a
Victorian garden inside the house.*

WHAT YOU'LL NEED

Distressed-wire basket

Wire cutters

8 sprays of silk gardenias

Floral wire

Floral tape

3 yards (2.7 m) metallic gold ribbon

INSTRUCTIONS

1. Using the wire cutters, snip the sprays of gardenias apart where the smaller stems branch off from the main stem.

2. Wire the gardenias together to form two sprays that are the same length as the basket you're using. Make sure that the size and shape of your arrangements are balanced. Cover the wire with floral tape.

3. Attach the gardenia sprays onto each side of the basket with floral wire. Secure them in several places, to ensure stability.

4. Weave the gold ribbon through the flowers and around the sides of the basket.

JOSS PAPER TRAY

DESIGNER: TERRY TAYLOR

Give a simple, split bamboo tray Asian flair with brightly printed joss papers highlighted with gold leaf.

WHAT YOU'LL NEED

Bamboo tray

Selection of joss papers*

Ruler

Spray fixative

Wax paper

Acrylic varnish, matte or glossy
   as desired

Paintbrush

Composition gold leaf and leafing
   adhesive (optional)

Acrylic paints, gold and red or orange

*You can find joss papers in Asian markets. Many art and paper stores carry these versatile accent papers as well.

INSTRUCTIONS

1. Trim the white portion of a sheet of the joss paper. Lay it on a flat work surface and tear it away, using the edge of the ruler as a guide. The designer likes the look of hand-torn papers, but you could trim them with scissors if desired. Trim as many joss papers as you think you'll need.

2. Experiment with the placement of the papers on the tray surface. When you are happy with their placement, set them aside.

3. Seal each piece of joss paper, front and back, with the spray fixative. Let them dry.

4. Place a sheet of joss paper facedown on a length of wax paper. Use the paintbrush to coat the back of the joss paper with a thin coat of the acrylic varnish.

5. Carefully lift the joss paper and place it faceup on the tray. Use your fingers to smooth out the paper. Apply a light coat of varnish, spreading the varnish slightly over the edges of the joss paper. If air bubbles form under the paper, use a straight pin to prick the bubble, then smooth it out with the paintbrush.

6. Adhere the remaining sheets of joss paper and let them dry. If desired, give the entire tray surface a final coat of the acrylic varnish.

7. Paint the rim with a base coat of red or orange paint. Let it dry. Apply leafing adhesive, according to the manufacturer's instructions. Adhere tiny bits of gold leaf to the rim.

8. Seal the coat of paint and the gold leaf with a coat of acrylic varnish.

VARIATION

If you can't find joss papers, use washi (origami) papers. Some have subtle gold details in them that will nicely complement the gold leaf on the basket's rim.

GARDENER'S GIFT BASKET

DESIGNER: TERRY TAYLOR

This gift basket is a perfect gift for a novice gardener. But a horticultural doyenne will be just as pleased with new hand tools, the season's newest variety of seeds, and lighthearted garden markers.

WHAT YOU'LL NEED

Tall basket with several compartments

Miniature clay pots

Small and extra large wooden garden markers

Rubber stamp alphabet and stamp pad

Glue gun with glue sticks

Seed packets

Wire-edged ribbon

Tissue paper or excelsior

Trowel, hand rake, plant shears, peat pots, and
  gardener's gloves

Basket shrink wrap and hair dryer (optional)

INSTRUCTIONS

1. Hot-glue the miniature clay pots to the top of the extra large wooden garden markers. Add them to the other items in the basket when you've finished it.

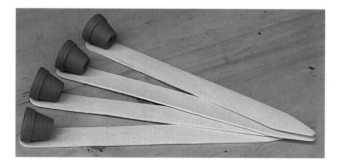

2. Rubber stamp the plant names of the seeds you've purchased on the smaller garden markers.

3. Hot-glue the small markers to the matching seed packets.

4. Hot-glue the seed packets to the basket.

5. Tie a simple bow on the basket handle, using a length of wire-edged ribbon. If desired, you can adhere the ends of the ribbon to the basket handle.

6. Stuff crumpled tissue paper or excelsior in the bottom of the basket. Array the tools you've purchased in the basket. Don't forget to remove the price tags!

VARIATION

To give this project a professional finish, use gift-basket shrink wrap (you seal it with a hair dryer) that can be found at craft stores.

Flower Girl

DESIGNER: CORINNE KURZMANN

Imagine a child scattering fresh flower petals from this charming basket on your wedding day. You can easily match the basket to your wedding colors.

What You'll Need

Green basket with handle

1 large cream or white silk rose

12 stems cream or white silk tea roses
(8 blooms per stem)

2 stems of apricot tea roses

Scissors

Glue gun with glue sticks

Newspaper

Instructions

1. Cover your work surface with newspaper. While the glue gun heats up, snip the rosebuds and leaves from their stems.

2. Center the large rose on one side of the basket at the base of the handle. Place a dab of hot glue on the back of the rosebud and press it against the basket for 20 seconds, or until it adheres.

3. Working outward from the center rose, glue the rest of the buds in place to cover the basket. Place the apricot-colored buds randomly in the arrangement as you work.

4. Use the leaves to fill in any gaps between the rosebuds and to accent the basket's rim. For a fresh look, sparingly dab dots of hot glue on some of the rosebuds, to emulate dew.

Variation

Loosely wrap a gauzy ribbon around the handle for a delicate finish.

SAFARI BASKET

DESIGNER: ALLISON SMITH

Designer Allison Smith's handsome decorative treatment, using African animal figures and natural tones and materials, makes this basket work in any room.

WHAT YOU'LL NEED

Large stained and lacquered basket

2 spools of natural jute twine

Long nail driven into a board

Scissors

Tape

Thin black wire

Pliers

6 small carved wooden animals
(found at an import store)

Glue gun and glue sticks

INSTRUCTIONS

1. To make the rope, cut 16 lengths of twine. The length of the twine should be equal to twice the circumference of the basket. Gather the twine into two bunches and tie a knot in the end of each bunch. Tie the end of one bunch of twine onto the nail, and twist the twine in a clockwise direction until it's very tight, as shown in figure 1. Tape the other end down securely so that it doesn't unravel. Tie the second bunch of twine onto the nail, above the first one, and twist it clockwise. When both of the bunches of twine have been twisted, hold them from the ends and allow them to naturally twist together counterclockwise. Finish twisting the rope until it's very tight, then tie knots in both ends.

2. To make the tassel, first wrap a very long length of twine 30 times around the middle of a hardback book that is a little longer than the length you'd like the finished tassel to be, as shown in figure 2. Ease the bundle off onto a flat surface.

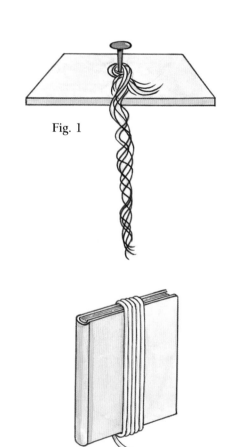

Fig. 1

Fig. 2

SAFARI BASKET

3. Referring to figure 3, place a knotted end of the rope onto the bundle so that the end of the knot is off center by approximately the length of the knot itself. Work the twine evenly around the knot, so it wraps all the way around it and covers the knot completely. Tie a piece of wire securely around the twine and above the knot. Cut all the way through both ends of the loops to make the tassel's fringe.

4. Fold the fringe down so that it covers the exposed wire and creates a tassel base, as shown in figure 4.

5. Make a loop at the end of a 12-inch (30.5 cm) piece of twine. Holding the loop against the tassel base, wrap the rest of the twine securely around the tassel base six or eight times, as shown in figure 5. Thread the loose end of the thread through the loop, then pull both ends until the knot is secure under the wrapping. Trim the loose ends and shape the bottom of the tassel. Repeat on the other end of the rope. Make a second roped tassel in the same way.

6. Place the cords so they wrap around the top edge of the basket, and tie them to each other in front and back. Tack the cords in place by wiring them through the basket. Hot-glue the wooden animals to the cording.

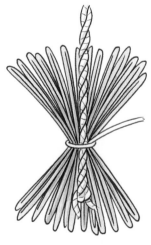

Fig. 3

Fig. 4

Fig. 5

Boudoir Soap Basket

DESIGNER: ALLISON SMITH

Fancy soaps deserve a special storage place. Strands of pearls on a string create a deluxe basket that show off your finest aromatic accessories.

WHAT YOU'LL NEED

Gold wire basket with a very open weave

Imitation pearl strands (sold by the yard or meter in craft stores)

Glue gun

Scissors

Vintage brooch (optional)

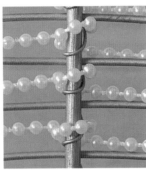

INSTRUCTIONS

1. Find the place on the bottom edge of the basket where the cross weave of the baskets begins and, using the glue gun, attach one end of the pearl strand there.

2. Weave the strands around the basket. At each vertical wire, or rib, wrap the strand around it before continuing.

3. Attach the end to the last vertical wire with the glue gun. Cut the string. Hot-glue a costume jewelry brooch on one side if desired.

TOTO'S PICNIC BASKET

DESIGNER: ALLISON SMITH

This double-lid style is perfect for carrying a casual picnic lunch or a small dog. Designer Allison Smith lined her basket with a bandana print twill.

WHAT YOU'LL NEED

Large basket

Fabric for 2 strips 5 inches (12.7 cm) wide and long
   enough to wrap all the way around the basket.

Scissors

Sewing machine

Coordinating thread

Iron and ironing board

Fabric to double-line the inside of the basket,
   plus a 4-inch (10.2 cm) overhang all around,
   cut as described below

INSTRUCTIONS

1. Cut two strips of material, each 5 inches (15.2 cm) wide and long enough to wrap around the basket. Fold the fabric in half lengthwise with the right sides together. Sew one end and along both sides of the fabric. Turn the fabric right side out by placing the end on the handle of a wooden spoon and pushing it through. Press the sash. Finish the open end by folding the raw edges under, and whipstitch (figure 1) the opening closed. Repeat with the other fabric strip.

2. Fold the remaining fabric in half with the right sides together. Carefully smooth and tuck the fabric into the basket to create a lining. Keep the fabric positioned so that the gathers lie evenly around the sides of the basket, and drape the excess material over the sides. Trim the overhang to 4 inches (10.2 cm) in length.

3. Pin the edges of the liner together. Use pins to mark the positions of the handles on the fabric.

Carefully remove the fabric from the basket, and cut between the double pins that mark the positions of the handles. Cut just inside the pins, making a 5-inch-deep (12.7 cm) U into each side of the liner (see figure 1 on page 94).

4. Stitch the bottom of the U cutout, but leave its sides open, as shown in figure 1. Sew the fabric together using a ½-inch (1.3 cm) seam allowance. Leave a 4-inch (10.2 cm) section open on one end for turning. Turn the fabric right side out and press it. Whipstitch the opening closed. Sew a 3-inch-deep (7.6 cm) pocket around the entire liner for the ties to slide through.

5. Attach a safety pin onto one end of a tie and thread it through the pocket. Remove the safety pin, and repeat with the other tie.

6. Place the liner in the basket, and tie the sashes into loose bows. Adjust the liner so its gathers are evenly arranged around the edge.

WINTERBERRY CHRISTMAS

DESIGNER: ALLISON SMITH

This basket is a great place to put Christmas cards or last-minute gifts for surprise guests. You can easily custom-dye a plain rattan basket yourself!

WHAT YOU'LL NEED

- Unfinished rattan basket
- Canning pot large enough to hold the basket
- Liquid fabric dye in red and maroon
- 4 pieces of silk greenery
- Floral wire
- Red eucalyptus
- Artificial holly berries
- Pliers
- Mini pine cones
- Glue gun and glue sticks
- Small silk bird
- Small ornamental bird's nest

INSTRUCTIONS

1. Fill the canning pot halfway up with water. Place on the stove over medium heat, and add a half bottle each of the red and maroon dyes. When the water comes up to a simmer, submerge the basket in the dye. Carefully turn the basket to cover all surfaces. Watch the basket, leaving it in the dye bath long enough for a nice, rich color to develop. The time necessary will vary among brands. Remove the basket, and allow it to dry on a flattened garbage bag covered with several sheets of newspaper.

2. When the basket has dried, create the base of the floral arrangement by gathering the four stems of greenery into two bunches, with the wire stems pointing toward the center. Secure them to the basket with floral wire.

3. Tuck the sprigs of eucalyptus into the wire that holds the greenery bunches.

4. Add the holly berries, and secure them with floral wire.

5. Place the pine cones randomly among the greenery to fill any empty spaces, and attach them with hot glue.

6. Hot-glue the bird's nest and the small bird to the top of the arrangement.

A Day in Bed

DESIGNER: JEAN TOMASO MOORE

Luxuriate in bed with this sumptuous two-handled basket at your side. Draped over one of the inside walls is a satin bed caddy that holds stationery, love letters, and writing accoutrements—leaving plenty of room for a book and your favorite hand lotion.

What You'll Need

Note: This is a great basket to make use of special vintage fabrics, ribbons, and trims that you may have collected over time. The lining fabric used in this project was once an old pillow cover, and the satin bed caddy came from the designer's mother's hope chest.

Sturdy, square two-handled basket, 12 x 12 inches (30.5 x 30.5 cm)

Light pink latex acrylic spray paint

1 yard (.9 m) vintage (or new) lining fabric (a silk brocade was used in the sample)

Scissors

Measuring tape

Glue gun and glue sticks

Straight pins

Sewing machine

Satin bed caddy, or 1 yard (.9 m) each pink and green satin, to sew your own

Several tiny pink satin bows

2 yards (1.8 m) peach wired satin ribbon, ¾ inch (1.9 cm) wide

10 pink or peach paper or silk rosebuds

Instructions

1. Spray paint the basket pink (or a color to complement your bedroom décor) and let it dry.

2. Create a lining by loosely draping the fabric inside the basket. Fold down the raw edge of the fabric as you adhere the lining along the inside rim of the basket with hot glue.

3. To make the caddy, measure the height and width of the inside of one of the basket's walls. Cut a piece of pink satin equal to the width *plus 1 inch (2.5 cm)* and twice the height *plus 1 inch (2.5 cm)*. Cut a piece of green satin the same size as the pink satin.

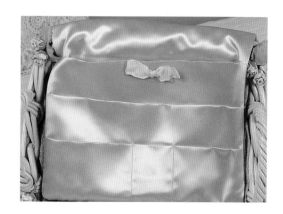

New Baby

CONTINUED

What You'll Need

Basket with handle (the one shown here is 10½ x 11 inches [26.7 x 27.9 cm])

Pastel yellow latex acrylic spray paint

20 diaper pins with yellow plastic heads

1 small flannel baby receiving blanket with elephant print

1 novelty-print handkerchief (for this project the designer used a vintage yellow handkerchief with baby-bonneted elephants)

Glue gun with glue sticks

3 yards (2.7 m) yellow gingham grosgrain ribbon, ⅝ inch (1.6 cm) wide

Scissors

1 yard (.9 m) pale yellow satin ribbon, ½ inch (1.3 cm) wide

4 wooden blocks, ¾ x ¾ inch (1.9 x 1.9 cm)

2-ounce (56 g) acrylic craft paints in pastel shades of yellow, blue, pink, and lavender

Small foam paintbrush

Alphabet stamps, ½ inch (1.3 cm), or a size proportionate to the wooden blocks

Stamp pad with black ink

Electric drill with small drill bit

1 yard (.9 m) pale yellow satin ribbon, ⅛ inch (3 mm) wide

5 pastel plastic pony beads

1 pair white baby shoes

1 soft elephant baby rattle, 4 inches (10.2 cm) long

3 yards (2.7 m) pale yellow sheer wired ribbon, 2½ inches (6.4 cm) wide

13 small yellow paper rosebuds (sold in clusters in craft shops)

Instructions

1. Spray paint the basket yellow and allow it to dry.

2. Attach the diaper pins diagonally (through the basket's weave) on the "front" and the two handled sides of the basket.

3. Drape the baby receiving blanket inside the basket. Use hot glue around the inner rim to hold the blanket lining in place, folding the edges down as you glue.

4. Lay the handkerchief over the back side of the basket, behind the handle. Place it on the diagonal so that half of it hangs inside and half on the outside. Add the diaper pins on the outside, as you did in step 2, to hold the hanky in place. Put a dab of glue on the inside to secure the handkerchief to the inside of the basket.

5. Glue the ⅝-inch (1.6 cm) gingham ribbon to the underside and outside of the handle. Glue the same ribbon around the entire outside rim of the basket.

6. Glue the ½-inch (1.3 cm) satin ribbon to the flat top side of the rim, to cover any gaps.

7. Paint the four wooden blocks with the pastel acrylic craft paints. Allow them to dry.

8. Use the alphabet stamps to spell out *B-A-B-Y* (or spell out the baby's name if it's not too long) on the fronts and backs of the blocks.

9. Drill a small hole through the center of each block. Thread a length of the ⅛-inch (3 mm) satin ribbon through the blocks, placing a pony bead between each block and on each end block, to look like the old-fashioned baby hospital bracelets. Tie the blocks to one side of the handle.

10. Substitute the same narrow satin ribbon for the shoelaces in the baby shoes.

11. Glue one end of a short piece of the ½-inch (1.3 cm) satin ribbon to the back of each shoe. Drape the ribbon over the handle, so the shoes hang on the side of the basket opposite the blocks. When you've created a pleasing compostion with the shoes, use hot glue to attach them to each other and apply another dab of glue to secure them to the handle.

12. Wrap a 12-inch (30.5 cm) piece of ⅝-inch (1.6 cm) gingham ribbon around the soft rattle, and tie it to the outside of the handle opposite the shoes.

13. Create a large, loopy bow from the sheer wired ribbon. Choose a style you like from the ones illustrated in Bow Tying 101 on pages 12–13.

14. Glue the bow to the handle, above the shoes. Place yellow paper rosebuds randomly on the basket, to further embellish it.

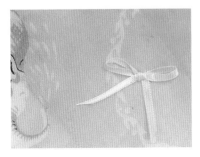

Wedding Memories

DESIGNER: JEAN TOMASO MOORE

Turn the bride's wedding mementos into a beautiful wall hanging—perfect for that first anniversary. The lace chosen could be a piece similar to that of the bride's gown; use a silk flower from the wedding ceremony.

What You'll Need

- Heart-shaped basket (this one has a blue colorwash)
- White or off-white latex paint
- Paintbrush
- Piece of vintage-looking lace (in the example, a piece from a bridesmaid's dress was used)
- Glue gun with glue sticks
- White feather and cotton open-winged dove, 5 inches (12.7 cm) in length
- Strand of small artificial pearls (available at craft shops and fabric stores), 45 inches (1.1 m) in length
- Silk magnolia flower with leaves, 3 inches (7.6 cm) in diameter (or use a dried flower from the ceremony)
- Wedding invitation
- Paper embellishment for the invitation, cut from a greeting card (optional)
- 4 cloth-covered blue buttons (in the example, vintage buttons were used) or use another item for "something blue"
- 22-gauge wire
- Wire cutters
- Green florist's tape

Instructions

1. Use a dilute solution of white paint to whitewash the basket; let it dry.

2. Choose a beautiful piece of lace to drape over the interior of the basket. Loosely drape the lace in a pleasing position over the inside of the heart basket, allowing the fabric to hang slightly over the outer sides. Trim the fabric to a size and shape that's appropriate for the basket you're using. Dab hot glue in a few strategic spots to hold the fabric in place.

3. Prop the artificial dove on the left side of the top rim of the basket. Position the strand of artificial pearls in a pleasing drape, starting at the left on the outer side of the basket. Glue the pearls into place; attach the pearls to the dove's beak.

4. Glue the flower into the lower corner of the basket.

5. Balance the arrangement by placing the wedding invitation in the upper left side of the basket. Dab a bit of hot glue onto a corner of the invitation to hold it in place.

6. Glue the four cloth-covered buttons onto the left edge of the basket.

7. If desired, the invitation can be enhanced by adding decorative paper elements with craft glue. For this project, the designer used snippets of embossed floral designs cut from a vintage wedding card from the 1940s. Pressed dried flowers may also be glued to the invitation.

To Make the Hanger

Thread 22-gauge wire through an opening in the weave on the back of the basket. Loop the wire through several times, and wrap it to form a circle. Cover the wire with green florist's tape.

PERICHO BASKET

DESIGNER: SUSAN KIEFFER

Pericho ("pear-ee-ko") was the name of designer Susan Kieffer's blue and gold macaw from Colombia. He was an amazing bird, and spoke English, Spanish, and some dialect of Colombian Indian. This basket is a little tribute to him.

WHAT YOU'LL NEED

- Half-circle hanging basket
- Needle-nose pliers or tweezers
- Spanish moss
- Macaw feathers
- Beads or shells

INSTRUCTIONS

1. Using needle-nose pliers, pull small strands of the dry Spanish moss through the basket weave from the inside to the outside of the basket. Continue until all openings are filled.

2. Insert some feathers through the moss, and tie on a small string of decorative beads or shells.